God Can Make It Happen

Russ Johnston

with

Maureen Rank

While this book is designed for the reader's personal use and profit, it is also intended for group study. A leader's guide with visual aids (Victor Multiuse Transparency Masters) is available from your local Christian bookstore or from the publisher at $2.25.

The Cassette Packet, "How to Live by Faith," based on the material from this book, is available for $9 prepaid from World Outreach for Christ, 1104 Cenotaph Way, Colorado Springs, Colorado, 80904. (Colorado residents add 3% sales tax.)

VICTOR BOOKS

a division of SP Publications, Inc., Wheaton, Illinois
Offices also in Fullerton, California • Whitby, Ontario, Canada • London, England

Third printing, 1977

Unless otherwise noted, Scripture quotations are from the *New American Standard Bible* (NASB), © The Lockman Foundation, 1960, 1962, 1963, 1968, 1971, 1972, 1973. Other versions used are *The Living Bible* (LB), © by Tyndale House Publishers, Wheaton, Ill., used by permission; and *The New Testament in Modern English* (PH), © J. B. Phillips, 1958, the Macmillan Company, New York, N.Y., used by permission.

Library of Congress Catalog Card No. 76-9215
ISBN: 0-88207-741-4

VICTOR BOOKS
A division of SP Publications, Inc.
P. O. Box 1825 ● Wheaton, Ill. 60187

Contents

To Dr. Ivan Olsen
whose faith and generosity
have helped hundreds walk with Christ.

Foreword

Russ Johnston is a man of faith. He is also a man of action. He believes that a man of faith should be a man of action.

His roots, like mine, go back to the Iowa farm. Perhaps this is why I understand and like his style—it is honest, forthright, and homespun.

The spirit of daring to trust God permeates Russ' life and breathes vigor into his message. I think you will find it refreshing and stimulating to your own faith.

When you finish this book, Hebrews 11:6 should have come alive for you: "And without faith it is impossible to please Him, for he who comes to God must believe that He is, and that He is a rewarder of those who seek Him."

LORNE C. SANNY
PRESIDENT
THE NAVIGATORS

Preface

I was 26 years old and *still* single. And I knew the situation was getting hopeless when well-meaning relatives stopped asking me when I was getting married and started wondering why a nice guy like me had never taken the step. But even though they had given up, I hadn't, and neither had God.

I knew that God intended to give me a wife. But He had more to give, too. He was out to launch me into a life of trusting Him to make the impossible happen. And the way He chose to work in giving me a wife was certainly in the impossible category.

I had started to learn about faith and trusting God some time earlier. Shortly after I met Christ at Iowa State University, I was invited to a Christian conference—one that would teach me to lead others to Christ. Just after I sent in the registration form, I received a letter from my draft board asking me to come in for a physical—the same week I was planning to be at the conference.

So I called the draft board and explained why I couldn't come. They explained that when Uncle Sam says come, you *come*. Otherwise you get drafted, immediately.

I was a sophomore in college, on a full football scholarship, and a new believer in Christ, so a stint in the military didn't seem like the greatest need in my life at that point. But God had said to go to that conference, and I went. And sure enough, I was drafted.

It took some faith to agree with God on His decision as I set off for basic training, but the time in the service was one of the best things that ever happened to me. Through the help of godly men in the Army, I grew in Christ and grew in learning to trust God—for everything.

I'd known Patti Brown for two years, but we'd never dated or taken the time to get acquainted in the way two Christians should before they consider marrying each other. But four months after I went overseas to minister to servicemen on Okinawa, Patti and I became engaged by letter, and a year later we were married. God had done all the providing.

These events were just the first of many in which God worked the impossible. In the early 1970s God began to do a new work in me about faith, and I finally grasped the truth of "without *faith* it is impossible to please Him" (Heb. 11:6). I'd been misunderstanding it all these years. I had been trying to please God wholly through prayer, Scripture memory, church attendance—all good things.

Faith, I realized, isn't just another of the good activities in the Christian life. It is the basis—the one essential—for hearing God's "Well done!" God had been trying to tell me through all those faith experiences that Christian activity was good, but the one thing He wanted me to do was to trust *Him*. Faith in Christ isn't just an additive for an extra-good Christian life—it *is* the Christian life.

As I started to share what the Lord had shown me—first in a Sunday School class in my church, and later in Bible and church conferences—I saw people stepping out to allow God to solve their problems and bring them to their full potential as Christians. And trusting God did more than just change their lives—it gave them a whole new way of life.

Believing God totally has transformed my Christian experience from a weary chore to a holy adventure. And it's happening to many others. You can experience the same change in *your* life as you learn to live relying on the God who can make it happen.

1

Getting Acquainted with Living by Faith

Jim Williams had a problem. A problem? He had truckloads of problems!

Jim, you see, was a total invalid. He'd been stricken with polio as a sophomore in high school, and the following five years in an iron lung had left him alive, but that was about all.

He could turn his head a little, raise one hand about three inches, and wiggle one thumb and finger, but other than that he was completely paralyzed. Only one-eighth of one lung was left working, so the exertion of even sitting in a chair would have collapsed the lung and killed him. And he faced all of this alone, because his parents divorced after his bout with polio, and they'd put him in an old folks nursing home to live out the rest of his life.

But then Jim met Jesus. And the Son of God took an obscure, useless life and made it a miracle. He didn't cure Jim's polio, but He gave Jim a life impact that's still affecting people today.

For one thing, Jim became quite a Bible scholar. This wasn't an easy feat, since the only way he could read was to have a tiny two-by-three-inch Bible positioned three inches from his eyes.

He also developed a real ministry of giving, which was pretty amazing for a man with no income. He'd pray it in to give it out.

And his zeal to witness put most of us who knew him to shame.

Since he couldn't go out and contact people, he'd pray them into his room one at a time to talk with them about Christ.

Don was a young collegian in the town where Jim lived. One Sunday his pastor stopped him on his way out of church.

"Don," he asked, "would you mind taking a copy of the church bulletin over to a shut-in in the nursing home across town?"

Don agreed to do it, but the "shut-in" he wound up visiting was Jim, and it wasn't long before you couldn't tell who was out to help whom. Don didn't leave the room that day before he'd heard about his need for Christ, and had given his whole heart to the Saviour. Today Don is working full-time in a ministry to reach collegians with the Gospel.

When Jim died after his third bout with pneumonia, the church was packed with people, including a lot of young college men he'd helped spiritually.

The officiating minister looked out over the congregation in amazement. "I hope there will be as many young men concerned with my going when I die!" he remarked admiringly.

One small, less-than-ordinary life had extraordinary results. And that's because Jim Williams walked by faith with an extraordinary God.

Now hopefully you don't have Jim's raft of problems, but you probably have other problems of your own. Or, on the other hand, maybe you're not hassled with worries, but even so you look at those God is blessing and using and wonder about getting some of those miracles for yourself.

How do you get God working in your life? All it takes is faith and seeking Him. Believe God, and you'll see Him solve your problems and take your everyday, natural life and make it a supernatural adventure! (Heb. 11:6)

God Will Solve Your Problems

Jesus was a problem-solver. He healed sickness, fed hungry people, raised the dead, comforted those who were sad, helped with decisions, worked on family problems. Faith in Jesus brought about those solutions.

And it's the same today. Faith—real, honest faith—in Jesus brings about solutions.

Joy had been a Christian a long time, but after a message on faith she went home full of questions. The idea that she didn't have to do anything but believe God to see Him work seemed too good to be true, and too simple.

"OK, Lord," she prayed. "You know my husband and I are worried about money." Joy was pregnant and had pressing school debts that needed to be taken care of, but her husband couldn't find an extra part-time job. She put the concern in God's hands, asking Him to keep His promise to supply all their needs.

That day on her way downtown she dropped by an office where she'd worked the summer before. As she was leaving, her former boss stopped her.

"By the way, Joy, did you know you've got some money coming from the retirement you paid in last summer?"

Joy protested. "I just worked part time. Only the full-time people pay retirement, don't they?" She found out she was wrong, and left with a check for $84.

She'd barely gotten home when her husband burst in the door. "You won't believe what just happened!" he exclaimed.

Joy gave him a big smile. "I probably will."

"You know that job I've been looking for? Today I got one. It's a counseling position, and it pays $11 an hour!"

Maybe your money is fine, but you've got problems in your family life. Ron and Debbie fell in this category. But the problem was with their family-to-be.

Ron was in the service and scheduled to report for duty in the field in two weeks. But the day he was to leave coincided with the due date of their first baby. The couple both believed God would have Ron home for the baby's arrival, so they prayed.

One week passed, then a second, and no baby. They knew the Army had no intention of changing its policy, so the baby's actual arrival would be the only circumstance that could keep Ron at home.

"Maybe God is waiting for us to step out by faith since we're trusting Him for this baby by tomorrow," Ron reasoned. So they drove to the hospital to check Debbie in—by faith.

Both hesitated in the car outside the hospital door.

"What do we tell them when they ask why I'm checking in?" Debbie asked. It was a good question, since military regulations prohibited maternity admittance till labor pains had actually started, and Debbie showed no signs of impending delivery.

They discussed it for half an hour, trying to come up with something to say, but decided to go ahead and try. God worked, and Debbie was admitted. Soon labor pains started and a few hours later their son was born with Dad standing proudly by.

God's protecting hand was even more evident when the doctors told them that there'd been a problem with the baby's Rh factor, and complications had just begun to develop in the child. If the delivery had been later the problems might have become really serious.

God can work in the problems you have in getting your family in the first place, or in caring for them after they're here.

Maybe you can identify more closely with a woman I met at a seminar, who said, "Russ, as I list my problems, I really can't come up with anything financial. My husband earns a good salary, and there isn't anything we need. But the place I feel a real lack is in my understanding of the Bible. I read it, but I just can't seem to get anything out of it."

I assured her that if that was a problem, she could trust God to solve it, because I'd seen Him work for others whose needs were spiritual.

Like Tim, whom I met when I was ministering to servicemen on the island of Okinawa. He'd been a Christian only four months, so I invited him to a Bible study. Tim was eager, but the study was scheduled for Tuesday evenings, and Tuesday was the day each week that his company was slated to go on maneuvers, so it looked as if he wouldn't be able to come. But Tim felt a real need for studying God's Word, so we asked God to meet it, and trusted Him.

The first Tuesday night, Tim showed up at the Bible study with a surprising story.

"Our company went out to the field this morning as scheduled, but we couldn't locate our companion company. We drove around for three hours, and it finally got so late that our officers decided to give up the search and come back to the base."

We praised God. The chances of losing a whole company of men on an island as small as Okinawa are about as great as losing the Miami Dolphins in the Orange Bowl.

The next Tuesday night, Tim showed up again. Because of typhoon warnings in the area, his company couldn't go to the field. For the first 10 weeks Tim attended every study. He exercised his faith and saw God solve his problem of getting into the Bible.

What are your problems? Are they the same ones you had a year ago? If they are, it's time to see God working on them by faith, because God is in the business of solutions.

God Will Help You Reach Your Potential

Some time ago I received a 14-page letter from a couple who had been Christians for a long time but had just begun to walk by faith. They were seeing God make of them more than they'd ever dreamed.

"Unbelievable and exciting! It's the only way to describe the change in our lives since we discovered how to believe God for our daily lives," Joy began.

On their way home after a message where they first heard about the living faith, Bob and Joy had a long talk about their Christian experience.

"You know, Honey," Bob said, "as I look back, I feel like we haven't trusted God for much at all. And I think it's time we changed."

They decided that their finances would be a good place to start. So the next night they sat down together and figured up how much they were short of ending the month in the black, and it came to $300. They prayed and asked God to supply the money, and committed themselves to trust Him for it. It was a first step.

Within 24 hours Bob had been offered two extra jobs he hadn't planned on, and the income from them came to $484.

Seeing God work so clearly, quickly, and abundantly caught them off guard. It was just the beginning, the beginning of seeing God continue to meet their needs, and then seeing Him develop potential in them they'd never realized.

As they saw God's goodness, both wanted to do something in return. So Joy approached her husband with the idea of quitting her full-time job at a clinic, so she might help other women grow in Christ. This would be a step of faith for both of them, since even with their combined incomes they rarely finished a month in the black. Bob said he'd pray about it.

A week later he agreed to the idea. But it was on the condition that they get rid of all their credit cards, and trust God alone for their finances. They took another step of faith, and God responded.

A girl at church came up to Joy after the service and began to share how discouraged she'd been. "I've been wondering if you'd consider starting a Bible study in my neighborhood," she said to Joy.

"That's really something that you'd ask," Joy replied, "because my husband and I have decided that I should quit my job so I could do just that."

The girl began to cry. "You didn't know this, Joy, but I've been praying for just something like this to happen."

Because of the girl's responsiveness, Bob and Joy invited her and her husband over for refreshments after church. And the couple opened up about the financial troubles they were in.

So the story about the prayer for $300 and a $484 answer came as a real encouragement, and the couple decided they'd try trusting God too. And they saw God bring in $40 through the mail that took care of their overdue phone bill the very day their phone was to be disconnected.

This generated some excitement, and Bob and Joy found themselves with a couples' Bible study. Later they started a prayer-and-share time for the young adult class at church to help some of them in living by faith.

The Lord had all kinds of ways to use them with which they'd never been in tune before.

A doctor's wife called Joy and asked her to lead a Bible study on Christ's Second Coming with some women.

"A month before this," Joy admitted, "if she'd asked me to do that, the answer would have been an automatic no. But because of all God had done, I said yes. And I never felt the power of God work through my life as I did that day. I've always been an introvert and usually go blank when anybody asks me a question. But that day I was able to answer all the questions from Scripture. This really proved to me that I could do anything God called me to, and He would see me through it."

The day Joy handed in her resignation, she put down as her reason for quitting, "Going into the Lord's work."

The personnel director of the clinic was curious, and wanted to know what she meant. And as a result, Joy got to share with her the Good News about Christ.

Joy said, "Had it not been for all that's happened lately, I wouldn't have had the nerve to do this, but God has opened our mouths and given us the boldness we've craved for years."

"We've always had our family devotions," she continued, "but they have never been really alive as they are now. It's amazing how many Scriptures have to do with faith, and though we've read them many times, we hadn't really applied them at all."

Dramatic changes occurred in Bob's life too. One morning he commented to Joy, "You know, if I felt God wanted me to go and help share this message of trusting God with people everywhere, I'd pack just what we'd need, leave all the rest behind, and be off by Wednesday."

He'd experienced complete surrender to do whatever God wanted him to do.

The potential for full Christian living was there all the time, but Bob and Joy never discovered it till they began to live by faith.

This has happened again and again. Faith does much more than just change one area of your life. It'll give you a totally new lifestyle. Faith just to help you solve your problems? No. You'll also become all God really intends you to be as you learn to believe Him.

Living by Faith

As you've read these stories, have you been thinking, *Why don't things like that ever happen to me? I serve the same God those other Christians do. What's the big secret?*

The "secret" of getting God's best isn't really all that mysterious. God will work miracles for you if you just believe He will.

It doesn't take struggling and striving; it doesn't take tireless effort in the work of God; it doesn't take hours of Bible study. It just takes faith.

"Without faith," the writer to the Hebrews says, "it is impossible to please Him" (Heb. 11:6).

It seems incredible to our 20th-century mind set that we can do nothing but trust God and that would be enough to please Him and have Him work, but that's the way it is.

Look at the lives of those heroes of faith (Heb. 11) if you're not convinced.

God called them something special. But He certainly couldn't have been referring to their morality.

Take Abraham, for instance. His wife, Sarah, was a beautiful woman, and Abraham was afraid that in the pagan countries in which he lived the rulers might kill him to get her, as they often did. So what courageous approach did he take to the problem?

Twice he deceived them to save his neck (Gen 12:13; 20:2). Though she actually was his half-sister, his half-truth was a lie because it was a deliberate attempt to deceive. God had to send a plague on the Egyptian pharaoh to rescue Sarah from adultery.

It wouldn't be hard to call Abraham a coward and a liar after hearing that story, would it?

Yet God called him His beloved friend (Isa. 41:8). And God used him to start a nation. If you'll check your history books, nation starters are a rather rare commodity. They're so rare, in fact, that three major religions claim Abraham as their father.

What about David? The Bible and Hollywood have both recorded in detail how he lusted after Uriah's wife, and after committing adultery with her had the faithful soldier killed to cover his deed.

Yet God said of him, "I have found David the son of Jesse, a man after My heart, who will do all My will" (Acts 13:22).

Or Rahab? There's no getting around it—Rahab was a prostitute (Heb. 11:31). She'd spent her life selling her body for money. But you'll find her listed in the lineage of Jesus Christ (Matt. 1:5).

Now these people couldn't have been honored by God for their upright lives or their tremendous morality. God honored them because they were people who believed Him—they were people of faith. As a result, they pleased God. When they got to heaven, God must have greeted each of them with, "Well done, good and faithful servant."

Many a struggling, self-sacrificing, upright saint, who kept all the rules and followed every moral obligation, won't get that greeting from God. Unfair? No, because God never asked for your duty-bound toil. He wants to fill your life with His power and His love and His goodness. The only way that will happen is by your believing Him.

What is faith? It's simply making a decision to act in light of what God has promised to do, and what He delights in doing.

If yours is a problem-laden, trouble-ridden life bogged down with unmet needs and unfulfilled heart's desires, could it be that you're looking down instead of up? While God doesn't promise a trouble-free life, most of us ask for trouble by failing to exercise faith. As you begin to make decisions in light of God's promises to you, expecting His goodness, you'll see God turn your ordinary life into an extraordinary adventure, because God responds to faith. Be prepared to see your problems solved and your potential realized, simply by believing God.

2

God Is All You Need

Remember when God spoke to Moses from the burning bush with a command to go to the Sons of Israel, who were slaves in Egypt, and deliver their Emancipation Proclamation?

"Who shall I say sent me?" Moses inquired of God.

The Lord told him to say, "I AM has sent me to you" (Ex. 3:14).

God knew that His name would communicate, because for centuries before and since the Hebrews had related to a God whose name was "I AM" plus whatever their current needs were.

When Abraham obediently took Isaac up Mt. Moriah to sacrifice him to God, he called God Jehovah-jireh, which means "the Lord Will Provide" (Gen. 22:14). And God had done just that in providing a ram as a substitute for Isaac.

Moses called God Jehovah-nissi, "The Lord is my Banner" (Ex. 17:15), after God had been a banner of victory for Israel over their enemies, the Amalekites.

Gideon named God as the answer to his need when God called him to free Israel from bondage to the Midianites. He called God Jehovah-shalom, "The Lord is Peace" (Jud. 6:24). And if Gideon ever had a need, it was peace, because his feelings right then probably more closely resembled terror.

Gideon wasn't a hero by nature. When God sought him out, he wasn't sitting around with a local band of revolutionaries plotting the overthrow of the Midianites. He wasn't even in the tabernacle praying about it. He was hiding by a wine press, threshing out wheat for his family and hoping that the Midianites wouldn't find him and thresh him out. No one was more surprised than Gideon when the Angel of the Lord said to him, "The Lord is with you, O valiant warrior" (6:12).

Valiant warrior? Who, me? Are You sure You're talking to the right person? must have been Gideon's thought.

But the Lord reassured him, "Peace to you, do not fear" (6:23).

Gideon chose to accept the resource of inner peace that God was offering him, and built an altar calling God his Peace, Jehovah-shalom (6:24). Not only did God give him peace, He later gave him victory over the Midianites as well.

The words God uses to describe Himself are not ethereal philosophies. They are down-to-earth, need-meeting words like love, Shepherd, bread, water, fortress, light. God wants you to trust Him as your supplier of daily needs.

That's why the Bible says, "Without faith it is impossible to please Him, for he who comes to God must believe that He is" (Heb. 11:6). God doesn't just mean He wants you to give a passive nod to the fact that He exists. Even the demons believe that, and shudder (James 2:19).

God wants you to make Him your personal I AM, the God who can be to you the total resource of all you need.

Hannah was an Old Testament woman who had the whole concept of looking to God as her total resource figured out. Hannah was married to Elkanah, but he had another wife. Surprisingly, however, that was not Hannah's problem. The difficulty was that Peninah, the "other woman," had many children and Hannah had none. She was miserable being childless, particularly since Peninah rubbed it in day and night.

But Hannah did understand one thing—that children are a gift of God. So she went directly to Him during the family's yearly visit to the tabernacle and vowed, "If You give me a man child, I will give him back to You to serve You the rest of his life" (see 1 Sam. 1:11).

She got up from her praying and went home. Her struggling was over because she had matched up her concern with God's ability to provide, and she was confident He would work.

The Bible says, "The Lord remembered her" (1:19). In due time Hannah gave birth to a son and named him Samuel, which means "I have asked him of the Lord." She didn't call the boy "My husband has given me a son" or "I've gotten myself a son." She looked to God as her total resource, and He supplied.

God Is More Dependable Than You Are

It's hard to grasp this idea of looking to God first for your needs because we live in a do-it-yourself age. If you need guidance, you go to a psychiatrist or take an aptitude test. If you're low on cash, you head right down to the "yes" bank or your friendly loan company, or dig into your pocket for one of those many credit cards you carry. If you're tired, you drink some coffee or take vitamin E. If you feel lonely or isolated, you join a sensitivity group or sign up for the "How to Win Friends and Influence People" course.

Don't get me wrong. I'm a Dale Carnegie graduate myself, so I'm not saying these resources are all useless. But if you depend on them alone to meet your needs, you can wind up sorely disappointed.

I heard of a counselor who told his client, "Have faith and you'll make it through this problem."

Jesus told His disciples not just to have faith, but to have faith in God (Mark 11:22). That's a big difference. It's possible to have strong faith, but to have faith centered in the wrong object, like in your ability to earn money, your education, your husband or wife, or yourself.

The Israelites made the same mistake when the Assyrians came against them, and they were rebuked by God.

Viewing the situation from a human point of view, it seemed logical that whichever side had the most chariots and horsemen would win. Since Israel came up on the short side of the tally, their leaders tried to work out a deal with Egypt to supply them with the needed military equipment. Most people would say their action was a smart move, but God had a different opinion about such a decision.

"Woe to those who go down to Egypt for help, and rely on horses, and trust in chariots because they are many, and in horsemen because they are very strong, but they do not look to the Holy One of Israel, nor seek the Lord' (Isa. 31:1).

God wanted to save His children, but they turned to a pagan nation instead and trusted in its protection. And God told them the result: both Israel and Egypt would perish.

A woman I know said, "We were so helped by last year's couples' conference that we would like to go back this year, but unless my husband gets a big bonus from his employer we won't be able to go."

She was depending on the bonus to meet the need, rather than on God. If God wanted them to go, He could work through a raise, an inheritance, a gift, or a solution they couldn't even dream up. God is full of surprises, so look to Him as your total resource; don't trust yourself.

God Is Full of Resources

Maybe you'd like to trust God, but there are doubts chewing away at your faith—doubts like wondering if God really *can* supply what you need.

A woman came to a Christian worker and said, "You know, every time we have a need, I just pray my husband will get a raise."

"I'll bet it doesn't always work, does it?" he responded.

"Oh, no," she answered quickly, "but that's because we have too many needs."

Too many needs for God to meet? The God of all creation lacking the resources to meet any need we'd ever dream up. Impossible! When Gabriel turns in his yearly inventory of the Storehouse of Heaven, the inventory sheet always looks the same.

It simply reads UNLIMITED SUPPLY OF EVERYTHING. God doesn't know what shortages are.

When David wrote what we call Psalm 50, the Israelites seemed to have confused the purposes of their sacrifices. They felt they were doing God a favor by giving to Him, helping poor old God out in His time of need. And He scorned them.

"If I were hungry I would not tell you; for the world is Mine, and all it contains" (Ps. 50:12). Earlier He stated, "For every beast of the forest is Mine, the cattle on a thousand hills" (50:10).

I know that cattle prices aren't what they used to be, but if you figured $250 a cow, times the number of cows you could squeeze onto a good-sized hill, you'd come up with a sizeable amount of revenue to which God has access. Then take that figure and multiply it times 1,000. And that's only the beginning of His wealth! So don't start wondering whether or not God can supply, at least until your needs have exceeded that figure.

One evening we were sitting around the table talking about how great a family ski trip would be. I finally had to announce that I didn't think we had the money to go on it.

"But, Dad," my 10-year-old protested, "we've got the checkbook!"

Talli's idea didn't help because she didn't know that I was the resource behind the checkbook. But her image of my checkbook is how you should see God. In His checking account are *all* the treasures of heaven and earth, and that includes not just all the monetary resources. It also means all physical, emotional, and spiritual resources to meet *every* need you might have. So when things look bad, and you are a child of God, you've always got the "Checkbook." "My God shall supply all *your needs* according to *His riches* in glory in Christ Jesus" (Phil. 4:19).

There's a children's Sunday School chorus that says, "God can do anything but fail." And that means ANYTHING. He can change people, supply money, alter circumstances, control the weather, give children, provide joy, use you to help others. The list is as long as the needs that you have. You need to quit thinking that

God has the same resources and capabilities to draw from that you do.

God Wants to Be Your Total Resource

Perhaps you believe that God is big and that He is fully able to supply all your needs. You know He is a God who can, but you aren't sure He wants to.

You picture Him as an Ebenezer Scrooge whose bank account is bulging, but who will probably give you a "Bah! Humbug!" when you present a request. You feel that He unlocks the strongbox only for the freshly scrubbed, well-behaved saint who has said his prayers faithfully, cared for the poor tirelessly, and attended church regularly. You're also sure you'll have to prove beyond the shadow of a doubt that your request is really a need, and not just a personal desire. Sometimes it's hard to tell the difference.

Paul warns us, "Do not be conformed to this world, but be transformed by the renewing of your mind" (Rom. 12:2). One of the biggest areas in which we need to renew our minds is in our concept of God. God not only *can* be your total resource, He *wants* to be.

God is a giver. He is a generous giver, an abundant, liberal, hilarious giver. He loves to give and giving is part of His nature.

James says that "every good thing bestowed and every perfect gift is from above" (1:17). So when your neighbors who'd been told they'd never have children find themselves expecting, or your Christmas bonus is enough for the stereo you had your eye on, or your oldest girl makes the tennis team, or you get to witness to your brother-in-law, that's the time to stop and think, "There goes God, being generous again." *Every* good gift is from God. Just because He isn't given credit doesn't mean that He isn't behind it.

We sometimes may think we serve the Great Tightwad in the sky. But the God of the Bible is the absolute opposite. "God" and "giving" are linked so many times in the Scriptures that you'd get tired of reading them if they were all cataloged. He gives courage, strength, help, and victory (Isa. 41). David says that you can count on Him to give you direction (Ps. 5:8). He gives wisdom and under standing (Prov. 3:19). Paul states that He "richly supplies us with all things to enjoy" (1 Tim. 6:17). Almost everybody knows the best-loved verse in the Bible, "God so loved the world that He gave . . ." (John 3:16). The list could go on and on.

Not only does God give, but He gives generously. Did you notice that Paul said He gives us *richly* all things to enjoy? He gives wisdom liberally (James 1:5), life abundantly (John 10:10), and grace lavishly (Eph. 1:7). He is the One who promises to open the windows of heaven and unload blessings on you so gigantic that there just isn't room to receive them (see Mal. 3:10).

A young man I know in Wisconsin needed two pair of slacks and since money was tight he told the Lord about it. But he added some stipulations. He's not a standard size, so he asked for slacks that fit him well. Since almost all his clothes were blue and he was tired of that color, he asked for colors other than blue. And he asked his heavenly Father to give him the slacks, rather than someone giving him the money to buy slacks. Then he waited.

A couple of months later he visited a friend in Minneapolis who said, "Dick, God has been laying on my heart to buy you a new sports coat. So if my offer doesn't offend you, let's go shopping."

Dick wasn't in the least offended and they went. A nice provision, but it still wasn't the slacks he'd prayed for.

A few weeks after that he was leaving church when a man stopped him. "Listen, Dick, a couple at the church have bought you a gift down at my clothing store, so I'd like you to come in and pick it up tomorrow." Dick came the next day and was outfitted in a casual suit (that fit perfectly)—in brown. Plus one more pair of slacks.

Dick was ready to praise God and count his prayer answered, but God wasn't through yet. A week later Dick got a big package in the mail from a friend. Inside he found two more pair of slacks, bermuda shorts, two shirts, and a jacket. He'd asked for slacks and received a whole wardrobe. God hardly knows when to stop!

I used to sell real estate and a certain sale that I'd been counting on fell through. I was disappointed, but deciding to make it a time of looking to God to work in my business, I asked Him to bless my real estate ventures. And to prove my trust in God, as James says, my wife Patti and I decided to give $100 to a needy couple we knew in the city.

This happened on a Saturday, and by Monday I had clients who wanted to see some houses. We found one they liked, so I called the salesman who had listed it to get some more information on it.

"By the way," he told me, "if you sell that house, I'll give you an extra $100."

I sold the house and the $100 I'd given to God was back in my pocket plus a commission on the house. That was just the start.

A friend had told me that if I ever ran across a house that needed some improving he'd be interested, and while I was looking with the couple on Monday I'd spotted one. Tuesday morning he bought it. On Wednesday another friend called and said he was interested in getting a home, and by Thursday he was signing the papers for it.

God didn't just give me another house for the one I'd lost—He gave me a week full.

Because God is a giver, when He commands you to ask He couples that command with a "you will receive" promise. He doesn't say, "Ask and we'll see," or, "Ask and I'll think it over." He tells you to ask and you *will* receive. As Jesus says, "Ask, and you will receive, that your joy may be made full" (John 16:24). Or God saying, "Call to Me, and I will answer you" (Jer. 33:3).

Love loves to give. In 1643 an Indian ruler wanted to express his love for a woman, so he built the Taj Mahal. If humans can express themselves so generously, you can expect that the One who loves you with an everlasting love will be even more generous in His expressions of it. All He asks is that you depend on Him.

If it's true that much of our concept of God comes from the relationship we had with our parents, I should have a head start in seeing God as a giver because giving is my parents' middle name.

Both my folks have devoted their whole lives to raising the six of us and helping us succeed. Even now it's unusual to go back to the farm for a visit and leave without an extra $20 in your pocket. We've found we have to be careful what we tell them about our finances, because if they find out we're short they'll try to figure a way to help out. When they visit us, our attempts to entertain them are never as successful as when I have some carpentry project going with which my dad can help.

"What man is there among you," Jesus asked, "when his son shall ask him for a loaf, will give him a stone? Or if he shall ask for a fish, he will not give him a snake, will he?" (Matt. 7:9-10)

When your child comes in from playing and is hungry, do you give him raw liver, or ground glass? The situation is just the opposite. When your child is really hungry and asks for a piece of bread, it's hard to keep from giving him the whole loaf, and the jar of peanut butter as well—unless it's just before mealtime.

"If you then, being evil, know how to give good gifts to your children, how much more shall your Father who is in heaven give what is good to those who ask Him!" (Matt. 7:11)

Bob and Ken are both missionaries now, but some years ago when they were college students, they were traveling from Iowa to Washington, D.C. They had no money, and since it was legal and safe to hitchhike in those days, they claimed Ephesians 3:20, asking God to do "exceeding abundantly beyond all that we ask or think."

One day they realized near nightfall that they were 70 miles from the town they'd set as their goal to reach that day. If their next ride didn't take them the whole distance, there was a chance they'd be stuck in the dark out on the highway. So they prayed.

They hadn't finished when a huge black hearse pulled over, and the driver stuck his head out to ask where they were heading.

"I'd really like to help you boys out," he replied, "but I'm only going about 30 miles, then I turn off this road. But you can go that far." They got in and wondered what God would do.

They hadn't gone far when the driver decided to try a shortcut he hadn't seen before. They drove for miles . . . and miles . . . and miles. Finally they saw the lights of a town. That's right. It was the very town the two had been headed for. God had gotten the hearse 40 miles worth of "lost" to see that Bob and Ken got where they wanted to be.

The last day of the trip they were waiting for a ride and recounting all that God had done to provide. Both now felt it was time to ask for the "abundant" ride, so they visualized what it would be. It'd be a convertible with the top down, they decided. But not just any convertible. It needed to be a nice one.

They had barely finished praying when a car pulled up beside them, offering a ride. Sure enough, it was a convertible with the top down, a shiny new white Chrysler all upholstered with black leather.

God enjoys giving to you. Have you ever read Psalm 23 and listed all the things that God wants to do for us? He provides, directs, feeds, gives rest, restores, comforts, vindicates, and on and on.

And it's because God is good and generous that His commands are not burdensome. If His commands are a burden to you, maybe you're trying to serve a different God from the One of the Bible. Maybe you've created a god who is harsh, unforgiving, punishing, or unrealistic in his expectations. This is the time to renew your mind about God and see Him as He is. Maybe you need to let yourself be loved by God. Lorne Sanny, president of The Navigators, says, "Let God do something for you, before you try to do something for Him."

God loves you even when you're bad. It's easy to believe God's giving nature to you when you've behaved yourself. Then you feel worthy. It's when you've misbehaved that your faith in His goodness and care gets shaky.

We can't believe that good things come to us *not* because we've done good, but because we belong to a good God. So when we've been bad and especially need God's loving care, we don't call on Him to help because we feel we don't deserve it.

When our children started picking up the little song "Jesus Loves Me," Patti and I taught them a verse that not many sing, but we all could use. "Jesus loves me when I'm good, and I do the things I should. Jesus loves me when I'm bad, though it makes Him very sad."

" 'I know the plans that I have for you,' declares the Lord, 'plans

for welfare and not for calamity, to give you a future and a hope' "
(Jer. 29:11). God is going to be kind and loving in all His dealings
with you because the goodness depends on Him and not on you.
You change, but He never does.

God wants to be your total resource. He wants you to live every
day with David's attitude: "Because the Lord is my Shepherd, I
have everything that I need" (Ps. 23:1, LB). And God is the right
resource to look to because He has all you'll ever need, and it delights Him to give to you. God is more generous than you think.

3

Rewards Are for
the Here and Now Too

If you're out to motivate people to do something you want done, the quickest way is to offer them a reward for doing it.

A real estate company in Colorado Springs gives a trip to Las Vegas to its top salesman every year. They know that company loyalty isn't sufficient to move people to sell houses, but a reward will. The principle even works on dogs. We found that our dog, Shasta, wasn't all that hard to train as long as the tricks she did had a milk bone dog biscuit at the end of them. Rewards are good motivators.

God knows this too. It's a principle He's been using for centuries with His children.

"Without faith it is impossible to please Him, for he who comes to God must believe that He is, and that *He is a rewarder* of those who seek Him" (Heb. 11:6).

I saw how God rewards us for doing what He wants most of all —believing Him—on Okinawa in 1960.

I was ministering to servicemen at the time, and three of the young men I was helping had heard about the Tokyo Christian Crusade, sponsored by World Vision, which was going to be held within the month. We talked about going, and the men checked to see about leaves for the 10 days we'd be gone. Don and Everett had no problem, but with Jim it was a different story. Jim was in the Airborne, and this was back when Laos and Vietnam were just emerging as world trouble spots. His unit had been on a 24-hour alert for the past two months, ready to move into the situation. And, of course, no leaves were being given.

Jim checked with the lieutenant in charge of his platoon about getting leave, but his request was denied. Then we tried the division chaplain. He was sympathetic, but the situation was so tight that men weren't even being allowed out on emergency leaves. And if any leaves were to come through, they'd be given on a higher-ranks-first basis. Jim was a pfc., and even if he'd been high ranked, leaves had been so long in coming that some of the sergeants were beginning to lose accumulated leave time. We didn't get much encouragement.

Tuesday morning was our scheduled departure, so on Sunday night we'd gone to the travel bureau to fill out visa applications for Japan.

"What do you think I should do, guys?" Jim asked. "Everybody I've asked says no on this, but I really believe God wants me to go with you to the Crusade."

I looked at Don and Everett. "Jim, we can't see any reason why you shouldn't go either. It looks like God will have to work."

So Jim grabbed a visa application and started filling it out. When we left the travel bureau we headed for Don's barracks to kneel around his bed and ask God for a leave so Jim could go to the Crusade.

Jim and I left the other two, and as I drove him home, there was a long silence. "We've prayed, but I don't know what to do next," Jim finally admitted.

I didn't know either, but logically it looked as if he'd have to get cleared from his company and have his leave papers cut the next day if he was really going to leave with us on Tuesday.

As soon as I dropped Jim off at the barracks, he started taking his field display down and packing his other things into his foot locker so it'd be ready to check into the supply room the next day. This created quite a stir in the barracks because word soon got around that Jim had prayed and thought God was going to get him a leave for Japan.

"Listen, Graff," one soldier hollered, "if you get leave, I'll really believe there is a God!"

"Right," another chimed in, "if this comes off, I'll even start going to church with you."

The next morning Jim went to his platoon leader to tell him he'd like to go to Japan, and that the ship was leaving the next morning. The lieutenant just shook his head. "Listen, Graff. I checked on this leave for you already, remember? And there are *no leaves* being granted. Get it?"

Jim looked the officer straight in the eye. "Lieutenant, if this works out, it will be all of God."

The lieutenant looked back with a big smirk on his face. "Graff, if this works out, it'll *have* to be of God."

A couple of hours later, a buddy of Jim's happened to be cleaning up in the D Company Commander's office. The phone rang, and no one was there to answer it, so he picked it up. "This is G-3 calling. Please pass the message that leaves will be approved today."

The buddy hustled over to find Jim and told him what he'd heard. So Jim went to his lieutenant, who checked at the D Company office. The lieutenant walked out of the orderly room, looked at Jim, and pointed his right thumb straight at heaven. He was so excited that he personally typed out the leave papers and gave Jim time off to hand-carry them to Division Personnel for processing.

When Jim took the leave papers in and laid them on the desk, the Division Personnel Officer looked at him with annoyance. "Why are you bringing me these? We haven't approved any leaves around here for weeks."

Jim tried to explain what he'd heard, but the officer held his ground. "Listen, soldier. If G-3 decided to give out leaves, we'd be the first one they'd call, not *your* company, because we're the ones who handle all the leaves. And we haven't gotten any word from them."

Just then a colonel walked by and overheard the discussion. "I'll check this out with G-3 myself," he offered. He checked, and sure enough, leaves were being approved. The word had gone straight from headquarters to Jim's friend, bypassing all the normal procedures.

Jim was so excited with what God had done that he began to spill the story to a warrant officer. "I don't understand this, Private," the warrant officer responded with amazement. "I married a minister's daughter, but nothing like this has ever happened to me!"

God had looked at Jim, saw a man believing Him, and had rewarded his faith.

How God Rewards You

Return a missing wallet and you'll probably get a money reward. For outstanding work your boss may reward you with a promotion. Have you wondered what God's rewards for faith look like? Are they cash, trophies, citations, or what?

The Bible says that God's rewards are not only crowns in heaven, but come to you in the form of what you need, what you're concerned about, or what you just plain desire when you're in tune with Him.

He's promised to reward you in your needs. The God we serve is the One who "shall supply all your needs according to His riches in glory in Christ Jesus" (Phil. 4:19).

Notice that Paul says *all* your needs. God never planned that you'd look to Him for your "spiritual" needs and be on your own to take care of the others. He had planned all along that He'd provide for you completely, everything spiritual, physical, and emotional, and every other kind of need you might have. Your job is to determine your needs; God's job is to meet them.

A few years ago I worked with a real man of faith, Dr. Ivan Olsen, founder of Maranatha Bible Camp near North Platte, Nebraska. It didn't take long being around him to learn some things about God's supply for His children.

One day he was inspecting the camp's dining room and kitchen when somebody with him asked, "Reverend Olsen, how do you determine how much you can expect God to supply of what you need?"

Dr. Olsen stopped for a minute, then replied, "In the beginning of Maranatha, I realized that this was God's work, and I learned that my part was to figure out what the needs were here and then take the appropriate action to launch out in ordering the items, or maybe start constructing the building. Every building on this camp complex has been started by faith without the money in hand. Because this is God's work and not mine, it's just up to me to figure out the needs, and it's up to Him to supply, be it finances, carpenters, or food."

It's your job to determine your needs, and it's God's job to supply.

If this weren't so, you'd have to be a very frustrated person as you read Jesus' command, "Seek first His kingdom and His righteousness" (Matt. 6:33). Needs are needs. You can say what you will, but a person who hasn't eaten in a week, or is about to lose his house because he can't make the payments is going to have a hard time really giving himself to the concerns of the Kingdom of God.

Now God knows that. He's the One who "knows our frame; He is mindful that we are but dust" (Ps. 103:14). God is thoroughly aware of your humanity; He knows you can't do two things at once. You can't be responsible to meet your own needs, and be free to be involved with Him in meeting the needs of others at the same time.

That's what the real message of Jesus is all about. Stored away in the middle of the Sermon on the Mount is God's plan to meet your needs.

"For this reason I say to you, do not be anxious for your life, as to what you shall eat, or what you shall drink; nor for your body as to what you shall put on" (Matt. 6:25).

Jesus goes on to tell us why we don't need to be anxious. God meets the needs that the birds have for food, and beautifully clothes the flowers. "But if God so arrays the grass of the field, which is alive today and tomorrow is thrown into the furnace, will He not much more do so for you, O men of little faith?" (6:30)

"For all these things the Gentiles eagerly seek; for your heavenly Father knows that you need all these things. But seek first His kingdom and His righteousness, and *all these things* shall be added to you" (6:32-33).

The difference between you and people without God is in what you give your energy to. Non-Christians spend their lifetimes striving to meet their basic human needs. It's the rat race of go to my job to earn money to pay for my house, and food to give me strength to go to my job to earn money to pay for my house and food to give me strength to go to my job . . .

But for you, the Christian, God wants you to give your needs to Him, and to expect Him to reward your faith by giving you all you need.

My friend Myron Rush learned first-hand that needs aren't around to frustrate us; they're permitted so we can give them to God and see Him work.

Myron had just moved his family to Grand Junction, Colorado and decided to build a home there. The arrangements he'd made with the builder included putting $500 down when the house was started, and then paying an additional $2,000 when the house was finished in June. The papers were signed in January and the carpenters went to work.

They went to work all right! Sixty days before the house was supposed to be finished, Myron got a call from the builder. "Good news, Mr. Rush. Looks like your house is coming along better than we expected. You can plan to move in right away."

It may have been good news for the builder, but it was disastrous news for Myron. He'd sunk all his money into a management training company he was starting, so he didn't have the $2,000 that he'd promised to pay when the house was completed early. So he took the need to God and asked Him to supply the money.

Within a matter of days the answer came, straight out of the newspaper. The President signed a bill into law providing tax rebates for people buying new homes, and Myron would qualify for it. The amount of the rebate? That's right, $2,000. Now I wouldn't be the one to say that God influenced the whole U.S. Congress to act in behalf of His child, but I'm not sure you could convince Myron.

Chuck had a need too, for snow tires. And in Colorado, where Chuck and I live, you don't get very far without them in the winter. Since he didn't have the money to get them, he prayed. After three weeks of asking God to supply, Chuck decided the time had come to act in faith.

Since a friend was going downtown, Chuck asked him to pick up the tires and gave him a blank check to pay for them, believing that God would take care of covering the check. When he got home from work and opened the mail, he found an envelope addressed to him with no return address, and $30 inside. When his friend dropped off the tires later that evening, Chuck wasn't at all surprised to find that the bill for them came to $30.70.

If you made a list of your needs, maybe your house payment wouldn't be on it, or snow tires. But how about your business? Do you have personnel problems, financial problems, or production problems?

The president of a construction company in Iowa had been hassling over his company's finances. He'd tried all kinds of things to get them operating in the black. Finally he concluded this was a need, and he wasn't doing very well in meeting it. So he gave it to God and asked Him to go to work.

"Within 60 days," he reported to me later, "the books showed us in good shape financially." God rewards your faith by meeting your needs.

Do you need good health? Or a solution to family problems? Or maybe some time off?

Several years ago I'd been under a lot of pressure, and decided I needed a short vacation with my wife. We were living then in Spokane, Washington, and a friend in British Columbia had offered us his parents' cabin in Canada for a "getaway." So I figured this vacation wouldn't be hard to put together. His parents used the cabin only on weekends, making it possible for us to spend a week there, and I called him to confirm it.

"Russ, I'm really sorry, but my folks are using the cabin on the very week you picked. I can't understand it. It's the first time in ages they've ever gone there during the week."

So I had to go to God with my need, since my plans to take care of myself had bombed.

And, of course, it wasn't long before a girl we knew phoned my wife, Patti.

"Listen, Patti. I was thinking of you and Russ, and realized I'd never told you that my folks own a cabin on the Oregon Coast, and you'd be more than welcome to use it anytime you'd like."

Off we went, expecting a wilderness cabin like we'd tried to get for ourselves. But when God meets a need, He does it abundantly. The "cabin" turned out to be a three-bedroom home on the Oregon Coast that was plush enough to give our house in Spokane a good run for its money. It didn't take me long to figure out that God was better at meeting my need for a retreat than I was.

God doesn't allow needs to come into your life to frustrate you. He brings them as opportunities for you to see Him work on your behalf if you give the needs to Him. God will reward you for having a need and letting Him handle it.

He will reward your concerns. Concerns aren't hard to define. They're those things that weigh on you, worry you—the burdens of your heart. David said, "The Lord will accomplish what concerns me" (Ps 138:8).

Nehemiah is a great example of God rewarding a man for taking his burdens to Him. Nehemiah's parents had been captives in Babylonia, and he had gotten the job of serving the Persian king as his cupbearer. This put him in touch with the travelers in the land, and one day he met some men who had been to Judah. He eagerly inquired about the state of affairs there.

The news wasn't exactly good. Jerusalem was in sad shape—the walls of the city were broken down, the gates were burned, and the people were just plain discouraged. Nehemiah loved his native land; this was hard news to hear, but he knew what to do about it.

He shared his burden with God, confessed his sins, and asked God to work. And God rewarded Him for his faith.

The king had noticed that Nehemiah, who usually was in good spirits, was a little down, so he asked why. Nehemiah shot up a prayer, took a deep breath, swallowed twice, and explained his burden for Jerusalem. Nehemiah admits, "I was very much afraid" (Neh. 2:2).

No one was more surprised than Nehemiah when the king said, "Why don't you go do something about it? I'll provide the materials. Go ahead and get some of your people together from here and go over there and build those walls."

It seems unusual that a ruling emperor would pay to have one of the subject countries rebuilt, especially by one of his captives. King Artaxerxes could have thought, *These Jews. Sure. They'd love to get their city rebuilt. I can see right now what'll happen. They'll rebuild the city—with my money, of course—then Nehemiah will lead the people left there to rise up against me. Anyone can see through this plot. Does he think I've got my head in a paper bag?*

But the king didn't see it like that at all, and he sent Nehemiah on his way. God had worked it out because Nehemiah did the right thing with his burden.

Bob, a fellow in our church, was concerned about his ministry. He had a real burden that his life have a broader effect, and since the yearly appointment of elders was coming up, he saw it as an opportunity to serve. But when the appointments were announced, his name wasn't on the list.

So Bob took his burden and gave it to the Lord. Two weeks later the pastor stopped him.

"Bob, we need your help. One of the church elders we just selected has decided not to accept, and we're wondering if you'd consider taking the job."

God rewarded Bob's faith and gave him his desire.

Colonel Dick Abel could think of no reason why he lay awake nights. His job in public relations at the Air Force Academy was secure and challenging. The war that had involved many other Air Force men was half a world away in Vietnam. But thoughts of the men being held captive by the North Vietnamese plagued Dick. Night after night he'd wake up thinking of them, praying that God would let him do something to help. Finally an idea came to him.

"I'll put in a call to the officer involved in arrangements for the POWs and offer to do whatever I can," he decided. "Then I'll let God do what He wants with it." He made the call, the burden lifted, and Dick began to sleep in peace again, confident that God was in charge.

Eight weeks later the office called back. American involvement in the war was almost over, and arrangements were being made for the release of the POWs. Dick was asked to help. Within 24 hours he was on a plane headed for Clark Air Force Base in the Philippines to assist in the preparations. God had answered his prayer. But God had much more in store.

The first group of officers was being readied to meet the POWs in Hanoi. Dick wasn't to be among them, but before the flight took off, one officer who was to have gone was called away by the death of his father, and another was unexpectedly transferred, so Dick found himself among those who would have the first contact with the prisoners held longest by the Viet Cong. At the Hanoi Airport, circumstances worked out so that Dick's was the first American uniform the prisoners saw when they unloaded from the buses that had brought them to the release point.

As the plane that was to take this first group of prisoners to safety was loaded, Dick went to get the bag of the officer who was to accompany them. But the officer stopped him. "Listen, Dick. I'm involved in the procedural changeover; you go with them instead."

So Dick boarded the plane to accompany the first group of prisoners home from the war, because he'd given his concern to God, and trusted him to work.

On the plane after the formal interviews, he asked one officer if God was in their thinking while they were prisoners. The man looked Dick straight in the eye and said, "Dick, if it wasn't for Jesus Christ we would have never made it." Later Dick had the opportunity of sharing that statement on world television.

When God rewards you for bringing your concerns to Him,

He'll do more than you need. Solomon had a big concern after he became king. He told God that He really wanted to be a wise ruler. When God rewarded Solomon for trusting Him, He didn't just make him wise. God said, "Behold, I have done according to your words. Behold, I have given you a wise and discerning heart, so that there has been no one like you before you, nor shall one like you arise after you. And I have also given you what you have not asked, both riches and honor, so that there will not be any among the kings like you all your days" (1 Kings 3:12-13).

You can't lose when God rewards you for having burdens and bringing them to Him. Concerns were not meant to be carried by you; God means them to cause you to turn to Him in faith so that He can carry them and reward you.

God wants you to believe Him for your desires. "Delight yourself in the Lord; and He will give you the desires of your heart" (Ps. 37:4).

God is a God of fulfilled desires. Just because Jesus said, "If anyone wishes to come after Me, let him deny himself, and take up his cross daily, and follow Me" (Luke 9:23), you shouldn't assume that God is sitting in heaven waiting to smash any fun ideas you might have. It's just that He wants to give you your desires instead of your struggling to fulfill them yourself.

How many parents take their seven-year-old's grubby little Christmas list and say to each other, "Well, now we know exactly what *not* to give him. After all, we want to be sure he doesn't get too things-oriented."

"No good thing," David says, "does He withold from those who walk uprightly" (Ps. 84:11). Do you believe that? If you do, you'll list your desires—make yourself an "I want" list—and give it to God, and you'll let Him give you those things in His way and His time. And He'll reward you richly for your faith. Of course, as you get to know Him more intimately, look for Him to shape your desires—even to change some. Remember, He wants only to give you "good things."

Fred Krebs had stopped to get ice cream one day, and while he was sitting down enjoying it, a father and his two sons came in the ice cream store. The dad bought cones for both boys, but it was disgusting to Fred to see how ungrateful the kids were. Their only response was to snap at their dad and at each other. But as he watched, it impressed Fred that, even though the dad didn't get thanks from his kids, it still pleased him to do good for them. And Fred realized he should expect the same from his own Father.

So the next day as Fred was reading the Bible, he stopped and prayed. "Dear God, I know You are a lot better Father than that one I saw yesterday. So it probably really delights You to give to me. And one thing I'd love to have is a motorcycle. And I'd like it to be a 2-cycle, and at least 300 cc's." He told no one what he prayed, leaving it with God.

On his next trip to visit his family, Fred and his brother were working together trying to repair the brother's motorcycle, when all of a sudden his brother said, "This thing! I've had nothing but trouble with it, and I'm tired of fooling around trying to get it to run. If you want it, you can just take it off my hands!"

Fred did. The cycle ran fine in Colorado where Fred lived. You guessed it—it was a 2-cycle, 305 cc's.

You're a person with needs and concerns and desires. The God you serve knows that, and wants you to give them to Him, expecting Him to fulfill them for you.

Why God Rewards Us for Believing Him

How do you feel about this truth that God wants to reward you?

I've had many Christian people say to me, "Russ, I like the idea that I need to look to God as my total resource and not trust myslef, but this teaching that God is a rewarder—wow! I don't know whether to believe it or not. It sounds so unspiritual. Seems as if it would be better just to serve God because He's worthy, and then if He wants to reward me, fine. But I don't know about *expecting* rewards from God."

This attitude sounds pretty noble, right? But here's the catch. God *wants* you to expect rewards from Him. God says that to come to Him you have to believe two things: that He is and that He is a rewarder. And in the Greek the word that joins these two things indicates that you need to believe both *equally*. It is just as important to God that you believe that He is a rewarder as that you affirm that He exists. He wants you to expect a reward for your faith, and if you aren't expectant, you're copping out on God.

Jesus expected rewards. The Bible says that for the *joy* that was set before Him He endured the cross (Heb. 12:2). Abraham was willing to wander around like a stranger in the earth because he was looking forward to a city "whose architect and builder is God" (11:10). Moses chose to suffer ill-treatment with the people of God because "he was looking to the reward" (11:26).

When we become children of God, all things that are His become rightfully ours, just because we're in His family. That's why Paul says, "You are no longer a slave, but a son; and if a son, then an *heir* through God" (Gal. 4:7).

A while back when I was speaking in Cheyenne, Wyoming, I asked a class of adults if any of them had ever received an inheritance of some sort from their parents or grandparents. One woman's hand quickly went up.

"Did you deserve that inheritance?" I asked her.

"Yes, it's mine!" she answered emphatically.

"But why is it yours?" I pursued. "Does it belong to you because you deserve it? Because you're such a good person?"

"It's not that," she admitted. "I deserve it because I'm in the family, and the inheritance was passed along to all family members."

God is free to be a rewarder to you because you're His child— you're born of God. But the inheritance becomes yours only when you ask for it and expect it.

Once while in Omaha, Nebraska I saw in one of the daily newspapers several pages of names of people who had dividends coming from their investments, but the people couldn't be found. The article was a request for these people to come in and receive what belonged to them.

What a tragedy! Some of those people might have been living in poverty and didn't even know they had money just waiting to be picked up.

Similarly, God has a list of those who have a rich inheritance waiting for them, and your name is on it if you belong to Christ. All you need to do to get that inheritance is to bring Him your needs, concerns, desires, and let Him reward you for trusting them to Him.

4

Simplify Your Life
by Seeking God

A senior missionary with one of our country's leading evangelical mission boards once confided to me, "You know, Russ, I see missionaries year after year get down on their knees and labor in prayer, saying, 'God, I haven't believed You in the past, but I'm going to in the future.' I think they sincerely feel they are seeking God, but it just doesn't seem to have any effect."

Are you wondering why it doesn't work? After all, God promises that He will reward all those who seek Him (Heb. 11:6). And doesn't it seem from all appearances that these missionaries are seeking God?

Does the idea of seeking God bring to your mind a picture of fist-clenching, teeth-gritting determination? Or maybe a recluse stuck off in a monastery somewhere in a slightly mildewed robe sitting in a straight-backed wooden chair, praying from dawn till dusk?

Maybe the problem is that we emphasize results—what we feel they should be. But God emphasizes seeking Him.

The Bible promises rewards for those who really seek God. David on his deathbed challenged his son Solomon, "If you *seek* Him, He will let you find Him," (1 Chron. 28:9). The same idea comes up again in Jesus' teaching, "Ask, and it shall be given to you; *seek,* and you shall find; knock, and it shall be opened to you" (Matt. 7:7).

Seeking God is a priority. The question is how do we do it?

Seek God in Your Everyday Life

When Jesus came, He began to use new words to explain our relationship with the living God. "Abide in Me, and I in you," He said (John 15:4). Abiding together—that's what a committed husband and a committed wife do. They live together, they share each other's lives, they're totally involved with each other, and that involvement grows year by year.

God wants to share His life with you, and in return He wants you to share your life with Him. He wants to move into your world and involve Himself totally in it—in every relationship, every business transaction, every meal, every bill, every family problem, every joy. *God will be as involved with you as you'll let Him.*

That's why He encourages you to seek Him. He doesn't expect that this seeking will be something you'll have to leave our everyday world to do; He provided a simple and realistic way to do it.

"Pray about everything. Tell God your needs and don't forget to thank Him for His answers" (Phil. 4:6 LB). What this verse means is *everything.* If God had intended that there be even one area of your life that you keep for yourself and away from Him, He would never have said, "Casting *all* your anxiety upon Him, because He cares for you" (1 Peter 5:7).

A missionary I know in Argentina tells about the time he was swimming and the button that held up his swim trunks popped off. He remembered the *"pray about everything"* command, so he called on God for a safety pin. Since he was close to the side of the pool, he climbed out clutching his trunks, and right beside him on the edge of the pool was one safety pin. Nothing is too small for God's interest.

A Christian wife told how she was finding the routine of her housework and taking care of her four kids just plain boring. But she didn't see a possibility for a change, so she took it to God.

"Lord," she prayed, "You know I love my family, but this

routine is getting me down. Will You do something to take away my boredom and make life exciting?"

Her husband finished the story. "Before the week was up, I was invited to speak to an adult group at a snow camp, and they gave me very explicit instructions to bring the whole family. And before we even got to go to the snow camp, friends of ours called and said they'd rented a condominium in Aspen, Colorado to do some skiing, but the couple that had planned to go with them could only stay half the week. So they invited us to come for the remainder of the time."

When God takes away boredom, He does it up right.

Sometimes God uses circumstances to remind us to pray about everything. During the summer of 1965 I worked with 150 college students in Europe who were getting the Gospel out. We tried an evangelistic coffee bar in Oslo, Norway, and it was a smash. We operated in a students' building one block from the main thoroughfare, and had packed houses every night with students responding to the Gospel message. Our plan was to run this coffee bar for three weeks in Norway, then to try it in Holland.

The location we'd chosen in Holland was as ideal as in Norway. We were to be situated in an old boat storage building in a resort area located between two lakes with great sailing that drew crowds every summer. Everything seemed fine, but there was a problem. It had begun to rain . . . and rain . . . and rain. One of the European news magazines reported this was the worst weather they'd had in 100 years, and that it looked like the tourist business in the area stood to lose millions of dollars since student vacationers were few and far between.

We could see what this meant for us. No tourists, no prospects for the Gospel. So we took it to God and began to pray. On the day we opened the coffee bar, the sky cleared, the rain stopped, and young people crowded out the town. Though there were cloudy days, there was no more rain in that area till August 17, the day after we closed the coffee bar. And the results we had were fantastic. To God alone belongs the glory!

The Epistle of James gives us a vivid picture of what we do

when God is excluded from our everyday lives: "You lust and do not have, so you commit murder. And you are envious and cannot obtain; so you fight and quarrel. You do not have because you do not ask" (4:2). This whole progression goes from bad to worse—desiring to killing, coveting to fighting. But it could have been stopped way back in the first sentence if after the people desired and didn't have, they would have stopped, and included God in their desires. They should have talked it over with Him—asked His thinking—and asked Him to provide.

This passage sounds like a New Testament version of the Exodus of the sons of Israel, which could easily be subtitled, "Grouching in the Wilderness." They had needs, some legitimate and some not so legitimate, but they handled both kinds the same way—with covetousness, complaining, grumbling to God. If they'd just sought God instead and included Him in their daily thinking and living, the story would have sounded more like rejoicing and praise.

It takes some work to remember to pray about *everything,* because sometimes it doesn't seem right off that you need to pray.

I have a friend who operates a paint store, and he'd found some used paint sprayers for sale at an exceptionally low price. When he talked to me about buying them, it looked to me like the kind of deal I just couldn't lose on. After all, I reasoned, he is in the paint business and would surely know the demand for them, and we figured that even if I didn't sell them right away I could get my money back by renting them out to people. The deal looked foolproof.

In fact, it looked so foolproof that I didn't pray about it. I bought the sprayers, and sure enough, they sat in the garage. No one was interested in buying them, and people to rent them were scarcer than chocolate chip cookies at a Weight Watchers' Convention. It was a good reminder to me that God knows more angles than I do, and that He wants to make my business ventures successful, so I'd be better off consulting with my Partner before I made any more "sure-fire investments." It was a lesson to me—as God intended—and I have not forgotten it.

Why seek God? We need to be clear on the why of praying about everything. The idea behind it is to open your life to God so He will be free to do whatever *He* wants in your life and in your circumstances. We don't pray about everything to get God's OK on our little plans. The idea is not to pray, "Now, God, I want You involved in this business venture or this family problem so things will all work out *my* way." We pray about everything so it will go *God's* way, so we're living in the center of His will, and so that His will might be accomplished on earth as it is in heaven. And that's 100%!

Seek God in Your Life Decisions

Because God wants you to include Him in everything, don't get the idea that He expects you to go into your closet for three days to pray before you decide whether to drive to work or ride the bus instead. God didn't intend that praying about everything would be a burden to you, but rather a help.

There's hardly a topic more tantalizing to Christians today than knowing the will of God. Many of us really want to do what God wants, if we can only be sure of what that is.

A friend of mine had a call from a Christian woman in her 80s, asking him for a ride to an upcoming conference in which he was involved. "I want to go," she explained, "because I see here in the brochure that there's a workshop on 'How to Know the Will of God,' and that's one thing I sure need help on."

And this dear woman speaks for many of us. Do you ever read with envy the Bible passages in which God spoke directly to people with a voice from heaven, or through a prophet, or with a sheet let down from heaven, telling them precisely what He wanted them to do? "If only it was that easy today," we mourn. "If only the Bible had passages in it like which house I should buy, or whom I should marry, or whether I should sign up for the mission field, or whether the blue dress is God's choice for me over the red one."

We care about circumstances; God cares about our hearts. We live in an age in which Christians are nervous about being out of the will of God. The high school graduate asks, "Should I go to Stanford or Moody? I certainly don't want to be out of the will of God."

The businessman thinks, *Wonder if I should invest in some new equipment or not? Sure would like to know God's will on this.*

The housewife wonders if the new house her family is considering is really God's will. "We don't want to get into something God doesn't want us to."

Most of the time when you meet a Christian who is wondering about the will of God, the decision he's facing usually has to do with geography or his vocation. And he's worried that he not get out of the will of God.

But when you look into the Scriptures, almost nothing is said about these things. There are, of course, some general guidelines. (If, for instance, you're considering marriage to a non-Christian or becoming a professional thief, it wouldn't be hard to determine God's will.) But on the whole the Scriptures have very little to say about whether you should marry Susie or Janie, Tom or Bill, whether you should be a plumber or hairdresser, whether you should live in Cincinnati or Walla Walla.

In fact one of the few places these issues are even touched on is in Jesus' sermon in which the questions of food, clothing, and shelter are brought up (Matt. 6). Even here you're not told what to eat, what kind of clothes to wear, or where to live; you're only told that God doesn't want you to worry about these things.

Does the Bible fail to elaborate on the things that concern you because God doesn't care about them? No, of course not. It's just that there is something God cares about *more,* and that is your heart.

Most of Scripture deals with what you are inside, and the effect that has on your outside style of life. God, it seems, is not impressed by those who do the right things on the outside but aren't with Him in their hearts. The Lord rebukes His people when He says, "Because this people draw near with their words and honor Me with their lip service, but they remove their hearts far from Me, and their reverence for Me consists of tradition learned by rote" (Isa. 29:13). The Pharisees, you'd think, would be "in the will of God" if anyone was. After all, they were the religious leaders of their day and gave up much to serve God. But God was not impressed by their religious vocation. He *was* more impressed by fishermen, tax collectors, and even former prostitutes who honestly trusted Him than with these men who were in a religious job and didn't have a right heart.

God is more concerned that you are living by faith and putting Him first in your vocation than whether you are a missionary or a carpenter. He cares more that you have a loving attitude toward your fellow workers than whether your fellow workers are engineers or a church staff. It matters more to Him that your home life shows His order and care than whether that home life takes place in a $50,000 house or a rented apartment. He cares more that you have a heart free from pride and covetousness than whether the car you choose to carry that heart around in is a six-year-old Mustang or a shiny new Continental.

Please don't think that you shouldn't ask God about these areas of life. Just be sure that you know what God's main concern is, and make that your concern. After you've asked God to show you His will about your vacation, your job, or your finances, stop and check yourself. Has the Lord already shown you some things He wants you to be doing that you aren't? Let *God's* concern be giving you the right decision, and let your concern be whether or not you are obeying the will of God that you already know.

A friend of mine at the Air Force Academy was telling me that he stopped by a newsstand one day, and a couple of magazines with suggestive pictures on their covers caught his eye. He was tempted to look again, but a verse he'd memorized stopped him cold. "This is the will of God, your sanctification" (1 Thes. 4:3). It was as if a voice said, "You *know* the will of God for you, Jim; it's your sanctification, and that means not looking at those magazines. Do you want to do My will, or not?" Jim said yes and turned his back on the magazines.

It's incidents like this in our lives that God is most concerned about. It mattered much more to God that Jim do His will in that situation. You need to get the same heart of concern that God has, and be more concerned about whether you're living in obedience to the light that you have already than in whether God will give you new light.

God wants to keep you in His will even more than you want it. The reason you can relax about finding God's will in your life decisions is that God is more concerned about showing you His will than you are in finding it. It'd be a pretty sad God who would give you a desire to do what He wants you to do, then take all the decisions for your life, lock them up in a storage vault, and hide the key, chuckling, "There, now. Let's see how he does at figuring out what I want him to do now."

Remember Jonah? God told him to go to Nineveh, so Jonah went straight down to the dock and hopped in a boat—headed 180° away from Nineveh. Jonah wasn't too interested in doing God's will. So did God dump him? No, not really.

God brought up a huge storm, fixed a dice throw, arranged for a great fish to swallow Jonah—all this so He could get Jonah to the place and the heart attitude that He wanted. If God would go to all this trouble for a man who was running from His will, just think what he'd do for you if you were seeking God's will.

"The Lord is my shepherd," David said. And just whose job is it to do the guiding, the shepherd's or the dumb sheep's? What does a sheep know about direction? They follow anything that happens to come along, and have to be watched continually so that they don't stray off. God knows that's what we're like; that's why God's rod and staff were such a comfort to David. He knew that God knew that he was just a sheep, so if he ever got off the track, God would be faithful to bring him back on. God delights in showing us what He wants us to do.

So if you're concerned about a decision, and you need to know God's will, remember that He's more eager to show you what to do than you are to know, and that takes the pressure off you. All you have to do is wait for Him to show you, and then do what He tells you to do.

How to Know the Will of God

1. *Commit yourself to doing God's will.* Lorne Sanny, president of The Navigators, did a study several years ago on the will of God. After searching the Scriptures, he concluded that most of

what the Bible has to say about the will of God concerns doing it—obeying it rather than knowing what it is. God's major problem seems to be finding people who want their lives lived His way rather than their own. When He does find one of these people, showing them what He wants them to do is the easy part.

God is not in the business of satisfying curiosity seekers, so don't come to Him to find out what He wants so you can decide whether or not you'll do it. Decide *first* whether or not you really want God's will. If you decide you do, and you'll do what He wants no matter what it is, the battle is 99% over.

2. *Believe God is already working within you to guide you.* Paul said, "It is God who is at work in you, both to will and to work for His good pleasure" (Phil 2:13). His good pleasure—that's what you want, right? If that's true, then you need to believe that God is at work inside you. He's at work helping you to *want* what He wants, and then, helping you *do* what He wants.

3. *Look at your heart's desire.* If you're committed to doing what God wants, and He's been at work inside you helping you to want what He wants, then it's time to remember, "He will give you the desires of your heart" (Ps. 37:4). Often God's leading is what we want to do anyway.

4. *Launch out.* You're committed to do God's thing, and you're trusting Him to lead. Then move out in the direction of your desires, and God will do one of two things. He'll either shut the door you're headed toward to show you another way, or He'll supply the resources you need to do the job as you go.

Paul launched out three different times to visit the Christians in Rome, but each time the Lord closed the door. And the door was closed because God was opening the door to other service that He had in mind.

Abraham launched out to Canaan, and God provided the necessary resources and reinforcements as he went.

When God appeared to Abraham (Gen. 12) and told him to leave his family and go to a land that God would show him, have you ever wondered how Abraham knew where to go? God didn't tell Abraham to go to a land that was 60 miles south and 84 miles west of the Euphrates turnoff. How did Abraham know it was God's will that he wind up in Canaan?

Look back at Genesis 11. There we're introduced to Abraham's father, Terah. Terah was the one who first had an idea about moving the family to Canaan. The Scriptures don't tell us what Terah was thinking when he packed up the family and started for Canaan. Maybe he thought there'd be a better future for his kids there, or maybe he was like the early migrants who went to California, thinking there might be "gold in them thar hills." We don't know. But we do know the family was on the way to Canaan.

They got as far as Haran, and Terah died. It was at Haran that the Lord spoke to Abraham and told him to move. Now Abraham was God's man, and he wanted to do what God said, but since God didn't say exactly where the land was he was to go to, Abraham followed his heart's desire, and headed for Canaan, following the dream that his father had given him.

We know today that he was dead right, because Canaan was the Promised Land. But Abraham didn't know that till he got there. He was merely going in light of what he wanted to do, trusting God to stop him if he was going the wrong way.

Living by faith! God's part is to be your total resource and to reward you. Your part begins by seeking Him, by including Him in your everyday life, and by looking to Him for those major decisions you face.

As you look to Him more and more, you'll find your life getting simpler and simpler. It'll just be a question of "What will You have me to do?" and then doing it as God answers you. And He will answer, because "He is a rewarder of those who seek Him" (Heb. 11:6).

5

Make a Deposit
with Phenomenal Returns

When God describes a faith that won't commit itself with action, He terms it dead faith, useless faith (James 2:26). That kind of faith won't take you far if what you're headed for is results.

If a man on your bowling team announces that he's sold on health foods, but when you stop off for a snack he orders a pepperoni pizza and a hot fudge sundae, you'd call his faith in health foods incomplete, dead.

If you say you're trusting God, put your money where your mouth is. Talk is cheap. It's the actions that accompany faith that demonstrate its reality to you, to others, and to God.

Make a Deposit with God
The Book of Joshua starts off with the nation of Israel poised at the edge of the Promised Land. After 40 years of wandering in the desert, it must have looked like paradise to them—green and lush, full of potential, a land "flowing with milk and honey." But between them and Canaan was the Jordan River, its banks overflowing. The problem was how to get one entire nation, along with its children, livestock, tents and possessions, across that flooding river.

As Joshua looked over the situation, he certainly didn't look to himself or any other human means to accomplish that crossing. If he had, the first thing he'd have done would have been to round up all the civil engineers in the crowd and start drawing up plans for a giant pontoon bridge. But the Scriptures record no such action. Joshua was trusting God alone to get the nation across.

Just because you're out to trust God instead of yourself, that doesn't mean that you wander around in a half-dazed lethargy just "resting in the Lord." Joshua didn't amble up and down the banks of the Jordan, waiting for God to make a way through. After God had spoken to him, his faith committed itself with an action.

Joshua told the priests to pick up the Ark of the Covenant and start into the water. Now that would take some faith, to begin to try to walk your way through a river at flood stage!

As soon as God saw the soles of those priests' sandals getting damp, He stopped the river's waters and made a dry road right through and the whole nation crossed in safety (Josh. 3:10-17).

That initial action completed Israel's faith, and God responded.

As one of my faith classes discussed this idea of adding action to complete faith, we were trying to come up with a name for it. I suggested calling it "Your Faith Pump Needs Priming," but one man stopped me.

"No, Russ, the picture is more like what happens when you put $10 in a savings account and expect to draw interest on it. The bank has the interest to give away, but the only people who collect that interest are those who actually go down and put their money in the bank. They step out and indicate by their action that they have faith in the bank's promise of interest. And they're the only ones that get that interest. Let's call it 'Make a Deposit with God.' "

He's really caught the idea. The difference between making a deposit in the bank and making a deposit with God is that at First National you'll put your money in and get only about 6% return, but in a deposit with God, you put in a little and get a phenomenal return. God will open the windows of heaven and pour out a blessing so big you'll hardly have room to receive it.

A little action of faith on your part gets a lot of action from God.

Jim and Karen had been married two and a half years when

they found out they'd never be able to have children, so they began applying at adoption agencies. But after another two-and-a-half-year wait, both were beginning to wonder if they'd ever get a child.

Then the Lord began showing them that He wanted to do miracles for them if they would trust Him. They'd joined the faith class, and at the first meeting were assigned to write down something they wanted to see God do for them during the quarter. They agreed together to believe God for a baby daughter.

Both now began to pray for the baby, and as Karen prayed, God brought a Bible story to mind. When the sons of Israel were stopped at the Red Sea with the Egyptian army breathing down their necks, Moses cried to God for help. And God promised that help. It was just the way Karen felt about their problem; they'd cried to God for a child, and they believed He was going to do a miracle.

But then God spoke to Moses again, "Quit praying and get the people moving! Forward, march" (Ex. 14:15, LB). It was as if the Lord was telling Karen, "Look. You've been sitting around praying long enough. If you believe Me for this child, get up and do something to show your faith."

So they did. Together they went out and bought baby powder and lotion. And Karen called her sister in Denver, asking her to send out the baby clothes she'd been saving for them, because a baby was on the way.

Within two weeks an adoption agency called, which had a baby girl waiting for them. Jim and Karen had committed themselves to believing God with the baby powder, lotion, and clothes, and their completed faith resulted in the baby they'd longed for.

This completed faith is the same thing that caused healing for the woman with an "issue of blood" (Matt. 9).

Jesus was on His way to heal a rabbi's daughter when the woman stepped out of the crowd that was following Him. She'd had some sort of bleeding or hemorrhaging for 12 years, and she believed she'd finally found the cure in Jesus.

Matthew tells us what she was thinking as she approached Jesus that day. *If I only touch His garment, I shall get well* (9:21).

She reached out for Jesus, and as she grabbed hold of the hem of His robe, Jesus turned around. "Daughter, take courage; your faith has made you well" (9:22).

Her faith healed her, yes. But it was a faith that was completed by an action. She didn't just sit in her living room, drinking tea and hoping that it might happen. She stepped out and took a risk. If touching Jesus hadn't resulted in healing, she stood the chance of looking very foolish in front of a crowd that probably included people from her hometown. She proved her faith by her action.

Norma had an ulcer. "I'd gotten to the point where I couldn't even take care of my family or do my normal household duties because I was in so much pain. And my disposition had gotten really bad. My life was anything but victorious," she told me.

But when she heard about what God could do, she realized that He had the power and the desire to heal her. So she decided that if she really believed Him, she needed to make a deposit of action with God.

"I didn't know what to deposit," she recalled. "But I finally decided that life had to go on. I had to take care of my family. So I decided to just go ahead with my work as if I didn't have the ulcer. And that'd be my way of telling God with my action that I was expecting Him to heal me."

So she went to work, ignoring the pain.

Three days later friends called and said they'd be driving through Colorado Springs that day, so Norma invited them to dinner. In the rush to clean and vacuum, her ulcer perforated and she was taken to the hospital for immediate surgery. In the process of that surgery, the Lord did just what she was trusting Him to.

In six days Norma was home with no complications, the pain gone. But the Lord did more than a temporary patch-up on the ulcer. During her stay in the hospital, Norma realized that she had the ulcer because she wasn't letting God carry the burdens of her daily life. And she decided that was going to change.

Six months later she reported, "I feel wonderful! No recurrence of any stomach problems, and on top of that, I've been able to turn every problem over to the Lord and not worry about it."

She made a deposit, and got the total healing she'd trusted for, though not necessarily in the way she thought the healing would come!

Why a Deposit?

The promises of God are usually coupled with a condition for you to fulfill. "Whoever will call on the name of the Lord will be saved" (The promise: salvation. The condition: call.) Or, "Give and it shall be given to you" (The promise: abundant provision from God. The condition: your giving.) You could add 100 more promises and their conditions to the list without trying: seek and you shall find; pray with thanksgiving and you'll get the peace of God; ask and it shall be given to you.

The reason promises have conditions is that when God does a miracle, the Scriptures indicate that He usually chooses to start with something. He created man from the dust of the ground, a woman from a rib, wine from water, a meal for 5,000 from five loaves and two fish, and demolished Jericho's walls by an army simply marching around them.

In your life of faith, God takes the acts you do to demonstrate your faith and makes them the basis of miracles. He used baby powder to provide a child, and the touch on Jesus' robe the basis for curing a hemorrhage.

A young Christian in Nebraska decided to trust God to get him some vacationtime at Thanksgiving from the barber shop where he worked. And he saw the need to add action to complete his faith, so he decided to send a $15 gift to a particular ministry. He was so convinced that he should let God do it all that he didn't even tell his boss he wanted the time off.

Later his boss approached him, "Bill, I've been thinking about the holidays coming up, and I wondered what you'd think of my closing the shop for Thanksgiving and the following weekend."

Bill smiled and replied, "It's your shop. You've got to do what you think best."

God took Bill's faith, completed by that $15 deposit, and used it to accomplish the miracle he was seeking.

What to Deposit?

Probably the most common question on the concept of making a deposit is what that deposit should be. It was the same question Norma had about her ulcer as she believed God to heal it. She had trouble figuring out what to deposit, what to put down on her healing.

If possible, deposit what you want to get back. In Zarephath, a widow deposited food to get God to return food to her (see 1 Kings 17).

During the drought that God had sent on the land, the Lord told Elijah to go to Zarephath, and a widow there would feed him during the duration of the drought. But the particular widow God chose was in a bad way herself. When Elijah found her, she and her son were out by the gate of the city gathering sticks to make a fire that would cook their last meal. They'd almost run out of food, and shortly they would starve to death.

But Elijah asked her to give the last meal to him, trusting that God would supply more for her in return. The widow did as he asked, and the record states, "The bowl of flour was not exhausted nor did the jar of oil become empty" (1 Kings 17:16). The little jar of oil kept pouring out oil, and the bowl of flour didn't get empty.

Her need was food, so she made a deposit of food.

Because the Bible camp that Dan and Phyllis were starting was a faith venture, their finances were low. And that was the time when their car decided to give out. So on the top of their "Pressing Needs" prayer list was transportation. Dan had a motorcycle, but for a family that's not the ideal form of transportation.

They began to discuss what to add to their faith, what their deposit should be. Since the need was transportation, they decided to ask God to send them someone with a need for transportation they could help.

That night the phone rang, and what started out to be a wrong number turned out to be the answer to their prayer. The couple calling thought they had the number of a local church, but somehow wound up reaching Dan and Phyllis. They'd been driving through town when their car broke down, and they were seeking help. Realizing that the Lord was working, Dan invited them over, fed them, and got the car running again. But just starting the car wasn't that much help, since the couple was out of money and the car was almost out of gas. Phyllis thought immediately of the $7—their last $7—in her purse. She gave it to the couple, who bought gas and left. The deposit was made.

A day or two later, a man they knew stopped by. "Dan," he said, "I know you have a motorcycle, and it's just what I've been wanting. I wonder if you'd agree to trade your motorcycle for my van?"

The Lord had provided just the transportation they needed in return for their deposit, plus throwing in a nice financial bonus, since the van was worth significantly more in resale than the motorcycle.

Norma's husband learned, too, to give God what he wanted to get back.

Chuck had retired from the Air Force, and since his work in the service hadn't really prepared him for a job in civilian life, he realized he'd have to start over in a new career.

After a month of job hunting, he finally started as an apprentice electrician, but it didn't look as if it was going to work out. The work he was doing was making his hands extremely sore, and an electrician who can't use his hands doesn't go far, so Chuck began wondering if this was the job God had for him.

As he thought about it, he admitted to himself that there was one thing he'd always wanted to do, to be a schoolteacher. But he'd never finished college and with two and a half years to go, he couldn't see any way of completing his schooling and providing for his family.

Chuck and Norma sat down together and figured out their finances, and concluded that his retirement and help from the VA wouldn't be enough to make ends meet. So they began to pray.

After they'd heard about making a deposit, both decided it was time to stop praying. They needed to do something. So Chuck deposited his job toward the Lord's providing the money to train for a new job as a schoolteacher. He gave his boss at the electrical company two weeks' notice.

"I've registered for college and completed three semesters," Chuck reported later. "Our financial situation is good; we have enough money to live on and the Lord has given us a continuous supply. By June I'll have my degree and begin teaching next fall. We are just amazed at how God works, and we know now that the only limiting factor of His gracious abundance is that we limit Him to give to us."

He deposited a job to get a job.

Deposit what God asks of you. Sometimes your deposit isn't hard to figure out. God'll indicate exactly what you should do, and your deposit is just an act of obedience.

An example is Jesus' first public miracle. His mother was trusting Him to supply wine for the wedding feast, so He told her exactly what action should be taken. He asked for jars to be filled with water, and when they were, the water was wine.

The Lord often uses His Word to let you know what the deposit should be.

Jim's mother had died, and he needed money to go home for the funeral. So he called on God, believing His promise to supply. As he sat in his office, he thought of a couple of people he could call, because he knew that if they heard about his need, they'd probably be glad to help.

"I guess it wouldn't hurt anything to at least let the need be known," Jim rationalized.

He started to dial the number of one of his friends, and as though a voice came from God, he remembered these words, "Wait for the Lord; be strong, and let your heart take courage; yes, wait for the Lord" (Ps. 27:14). God was telling him just what deposit to make to complete his faith. He needed to deposit waiting.

Soon a friend called Jim. "I just heard about your mom, Jim.

I wondered if I could give you a ride home so you can get ready for the trip. And I figure you must have some financial needs, having to go home so suddenly, so I'd like to help you out with that, too."

Jim obeyed, and God accepted that obedience as an action that completed his faith.

You can deposit money. Ask Cecil Piper if you want encouragement to make money your faith deposit to God.

Cecil and his wife had been praying for his brother's salvation, and believing God to bring him to Christ.

"It's time now to make a deposit with God for my brother's salvation," Cecil decided. He knew his brother had some needs, so he took $100 and put it in the mail with a note which said, "From Jesus."

Later, the Pipers' grandmother died, and Cecil met his brother at the funeral service. Afterward, the Lord opened up a special opportunity for Cecil to share the Gospel, and he led his brother to Christ.

I asked Cecil, "Was it worth the $100 to see your brother receive Christ?"

He laughed. "It sure was!" he exclaimed.

Because Cecil and his wife were willing to add to their faith, it became alive and dynamic, and God worked for them.

A man in a neighborhood Bible study I was leading learned for the first time about completing his faith by making a deposit with God. I'd shared with the group that I'd be teaching a faith course at a Christian institute in town, and that the institute had a $10 registration fee. The man came up to me after the study with a $20 bill.

"Here, Russ. This is to pay for the registrations for two people to take the faith course. And it's a deposit with God to sell my home."

His house, I found out, was 20 years old, and he was trying to sell it at a time when there were 2,900 other houses on the market. It looked hopeless. Later, God did sell the house through regular channels. And the week his house sold, only 50 other houses were sold, and for the Colorado Springs area, 100 houses a week was considered a very slow week. On top of that, the house sold for $2,500 more than it possibly could, so said three different realtors who went through it.

God took a $20 deposit and made it mushroom.

Almost any deposit you want to make will work. That's right. Almost any action deposit you want to add to your faith will work. Because the deposit isn't what gets God to act. Faith does.

When the woman with the issue of blood was healed, Jesus didn't say, "Your touch on My garment has made you whole." He said, "Your faith has made you whole." Just because a $20 gift got a man's house sold for more than he planned, don't think that shooting $20 to a missionary is a foolproof way to get your house sold. It's not the deposit you trust, it's God. The deposit just finishes that faith commitment.

Fred and his wife had been trying unsuccessfully for four years to have a baby. They'd had medical checks, and had followed advice given by doctors. When they heard about faith completed by action, both decided maybe God would work for them.

So they asked God for a baby, and completed their faith by sending $12 a month toward the support of an orphan in Haiti. Two months after the checks started going in, Fred's wife became pregnant.

Notice, though, that it was a different kind of deposit than baby powder that got them their baby. The *kind* of deposit doesn't matter, as long as your faith is being completed by action.

Don't Try to Work God Out of a Job

Remember, making a deposit means that you work a little and God works a lot. Don't let this idea of adding an action to your faith grow into self-effort.

A woman I met in Nebraska was asking God to give her a trip to Taiwan to visit her son. This was quite a step of faith, since she was an older woman and worked only two days a week. Her income was limited. But she decided God's income wasn't limited, so she looked to Him for the trip.

I asked her what she'd deposited with God to complete her faith.

"I'd decided to send $15 to a missionary," she responded. "But you know, Russ, sending that $15 off was awfully hard to do. I really wanted to put it in the bank instead to start saving for the trip; somehow that seemed more sensible. But I decided that if I sent it to the missionary instead, it'd be clear to me and everyone else that if God didn't provide that trip, there'd be no way I could humanly bring it about."

God did provide in some marvelous and unusual ways, and she flew to the Orient for a visit with her son.

If your need is a $300 dishwasher, and the deposit you make is to take $30 out of your paycheck for the next 10 weeks to pay for it, then that venture is not by faith. Neither is that action a faith deposit. It is more like trusting yourself.

A real faith deposit is one in which your venture is doomed to failure unless God intervenes.

Any engineer will tell you that walking around a city for seven days is no way to make the city walls fall down. Neither is stepping into a flooding river a way to get the waters to open up. You don't have to go to medical school to know that increasing your workload isn't the way to cure an ulcer.

Unless God had intervened in these actions, they would have failed to do the job.

If you're out to do a natural work, rely on natural means. But if you're after supernatural results, then expect to use means that won't work in the natural realm.

When you do a little, God does a lot, if your little is a completion of faith.

Do you want God to do great things in and for you? Then believe Him, and complete your faith with an action. God will take your action and make of it the miracle you desire. You'll have made a deposit with phenomenal returns.

6

Live Expectantly

That which delights the heart of God more than many other things is a person with an expectant spirit, a person who is really assured that God is going to do what He says He will. Assurance is a trapeze artist without a safety net beneath him. It's David sleeping like a baby with the armies of Saul all around him ready to do him in. It's boarding a 747 without a parachute tucked under your arm.

Assured. Expectant. That's the kind of man Abraham was. And a time when he clearly exhibited his expectancy was when God told him to take his son Isaac, and offer him as a sacrifice (Gen. 22).

Isaac was Abraham's only son by Sarah, and the son of his old age. It isn't hard to picture the special relationship that must have existed between them. Isaac had to be Abraham's most treasured possession. But Isaac was to Abraham a great deal more than just a "chip off the old block." Years before God had promised Abraham that he would be the father of a great nation. And you can't make a nation without people. So Isaac was the beginning of the fulfillment of Abraham's life dream, his calling from God.

Now God asked him to sacrifice the boy, to kill him as an offering. God had promised a nation, yet He was telling him to destroy the only beginning toward that nation in 100 years. If there was ever a time to doubt God's purpose or His plan, this was it. It'd be like God telling you He was planning to make you president of General Motors, and He works a miracle to get you a vice-presidency with the company; then He comes to you with a command to quit your job. Humanly speaking, it'd be hard to expect that He was still going to make you the General Motors president.

Abraham believed that God was going to remain true to His promise, so he must have concluded that since God was asking him to kill the boy, He must be planning to raise him from the dead.

Abraham and Isaac came to the mountain where the sacrifice was to take place, having brought along two young men, probably servants. When they started on their trek to the top, Abraham turned and said to the young men, "Stay here with the donkey, and I and the lad will go yonder; and we will worship and return to you" (Gen. 22:5).

Abraham declared that he and the boy would go, and he *and* the boy would return. Even though he fully intended to kill Isaac in obedience to God's command, he expected God to bring him back to life. He was expectant enough to commit himself before the servants that *both* of them would return. That's an expectant spirit. And it's part of the reason that Abraham was called a friend of God.

Expectancy. It's the attitude you need after you've stepped out by faith, and the attitude that needs to carry you clear through to the completion of God's promises.

Jesus said, "Whoever says to this mountain, 'Be taken up and cast into the sea,' and does not doubt in his heart, but believes that what he says is going to happen, it shall be granted him" (Mark 11:23).

The only stipulation for moving the mountain is expectancy instead of doubt.

Maybe you tend to be more like the woman who read this

verse while vacationing in the Rockies, and decided to give it a try.

She knelt down and began to pray, "Lord, that mountain outside my window. You said You could pick it up and drop it into the Pacific, so I'm asking You to do that."

Then she raised her head, got up from her knees, and ran to the window. The mountain was still there. "Ha!" she said disgustedly. "I knew it wouldn't work."

She *knew* it wouldn't, and it didn't.

Faith has tremendous power, but so does doubt. Doubt can keep you from starting out in a faith venture; or once you've started, doubt can keep you from finishing.

Have you ever known a person who is about as stable spiritually as a paper cup in the middle of a hurricane? Today he's fired up about this or that he's trusting God to do, but tomorrow he's thrown the whole thing over. Have you wondered what this problem was? James warns about the cause of that kind of behavior, and the result of it.

"If any of you lacks wisdom, let him ask of God . . . But let him ask in faith without any doubting, for the one who doubts is like the surf of the sea driven and tossed by the wind. For let not that man expect that he will receive anything from the Lord" (James 1:5-7).

Doubt is powerful business. Doubt can make you unstable, uncertain, and vulnerable to your shifting feelings and attacks of Satan. Doubt can take away your joy and destroy your fellowship with God. And it can keep God from doing for you what He wants to do.

So understanding doubt—where it comes from—and what to do about it is vital to living expectantly.

What Causes Doubts?

Doubt can be caused by fear, by the negative influence of other people, and by the frontal attack of the devil.

Fear will make you doubt. Doubt and fear are destructive partners; if one can't get you to question God, the other certainly will.

You're familiar with fear. It raises its ugly head every time you hear yourself starting a sentence with, "What if . . . ?"

Maybe you're afraid for your reputation. *What if this doesn't work out?* you say to yourself. *What'll people say? I'll get the reputation of being a nut, or one of those spiritually overboard types.*

We're all susceptible to that. It was concern for my reputation that made it hard to follow God's leading when I was looking for a place to house my family after we moved to the Northwest.

We had spent six long weeks looking for a house to rent. And during that time my wife, two children, and I stayed in a small apartment with a couple we knew. The space was cramped and the pressure was on. So when a particular house became available, I signed the rental contract.

But as soon as the decision was made, the Lord gave me no peace about it. As I was driving home one day, I told Him, "Lord, if You give me any evidence that this house isn't Your will for us, I'll get out of it."

That night I woke up in the middle of the night with Colossians 3:15 on my mind, "Let the peace of Christ rule in your hearts." God was trying to tell me that I didn't need more evidence that the house was the wrong one for us; He'd already spoken through my lack of peace. So I was committed to change.

But the hard thing about backing out of the contract was what the owner of the house was going to think. After all, I was a Christian worker, and I didn't want to get a reputation in town of being a fly-by-night who didn't stick to his decisions. But I had to obey God, so I went to the owner and told him that even if it meant losing my deposit, I had to get out of the contract.

It later turned out that the Lord was trying to tell us that we'd chosen the wrong city in which to locate. If I'd listened to my fear instead of trusting God for my reputation, we'd have missed a whole stack of blessings the Lord had in store.

It's easy to forget in this people-pleasing, image-conscious world of ours that the Lord you serve made Himself of no reputation. He was called a drunkard and a glutton (Matt. 11:19). And John the Baptist was accused of being possessed by a demon (Matt. 11:18).

Maybe your fear is the fear of failing, and that causes you to doubt God. "What if God doesn't provide the money I need? My family may have to go on welfare."/"What if I witness to my boss and he doesn't respond? I could lose my job."

That's the same logic Saul used when God told him to wait for Samuel to come and offer sacrifices to God. But when Samuel didn't show up on time (Saul's time, that is), Saul disobeyed God and offered the sacrifices himself.

"I have sinned . . . because I feared the people," he said later (1 Sam. 15:24).

What he feared was that if he didn't go ahead and take charge of the situation the way the people wanted him to, he might lose face in their eyes. They might even conclude he wasn't all that decisive, and maybe even go so far as taking his kingdom away from him. So to protect himself from failing as a leader, Saul disobeyed God, and it cost him the very thing he sinned to protect —his kingdom. Saul's fear of failure caused him ultimately to fail.

God never gives any promises of success or victory to doubters. So if you fear failing, then doubt God, and all your fears will come true, because doubting God is the surest way to fail.

"God has not given us a spirit of timidity, but of power and love and discipline" (2 Tim. 1:7).

Other people can cause us to doubt. One of the best, or maybe the worst, doubt-causers is other people. Often they're well-meaning people who care about you. They can be friends and family. They can even be Christian brothers. But they're looking through the eyes of human perspective rather than with the eyes of faith.

That's what happened when we were planning an evangelistic outreach in Old Losdrecht, Holland. When we first told the Christians of that town what we were going to do, their response was that it'd never work.

They told us that they'd already tried the coffeehouse idea to reach students. They'd even used the same building down on the wharf that we were planning to use, and no one had come. When we suggested that we'd be showing a Billy Graham film and having those who responded fill out cards with their names and addresses so counselors could contact them in their homes, our Christian friends were horrified. "You just don't understand the Dutch," they protested. "They'll never fill out those cards."

Well, we did have the coffeehouse, and saw many students trust the Saviour. We did show the film, and we had so many interest cards signed that we didn't have enough counselors to go and see all the responsive ones. So we finally had to resort to just inviting them to a group meeting where the Gospel was explained.

Christian people are sometimes those who'll keep you from looking at why God won't work instead of why He will.

I've been guilty of the same thing.

Warren Starr was the youngest college newspaper editor in the Northwest when he took over the *Campus Crier,* the paper at Central Washington State College. A few months before he became the editor during his freshman year, he had met Christ. So he decided that he wanted his position as editor to be used to get the Gospel out to all the students on campus.

One day, while we were talking, he shared an idea with me.

"I've been thinking, Russ. I read this article in *Decision* magazine by Billy Graham about how to get to heaven. It's written in real down-to-earth language, so I think it'd really communicate to students. I was thinking how great it'd be to have this published as a full page ad in the *Crier.* So I'm going to go around to all the churches in town and ask if they'd pay a share in getting this in the paper."

I winced. I knew from experience how hard it is to get churches to cooperate, especially when the issue deals with money. I started to explain all this to Warren so he could see that it'd never work, but the Lord stopped me just in time. It was as clear as though a voice from heaven spoke to me, and the Lord said, "Shut up, Russ, and let him try."

A month later the *Crier* carried a full-page ad on "How to Get to Heaven," sponsored by local Christian groups. Because of

Warren's faith, the majority of the students on the campus were exposed to a clear presentation of the Gospel.

It's interesting to note that when the children of Israel marched around the walls of Jericho, God didn't allow them to talk. Could it be that in seven days they might have talked each other out of an answer from God? They might well have all quit on the fourth day and gone home.

The Bible says that your leaders are to be those whose *faith* you can follow (Heb. 13:7). So choose those to follow who are people of faith, and who'll encourage you to expectancy instead of doubt.

The Devil is a doubt-bringer. Let's not forget that the devil is the one who started all this doubt business in the first place when he came to Eve and asked, "Has God said . . . ?" (Gen 3:1) He was the first one to replace trust with questions about God's goodness and His credibility.

"If God was really good, why won't He let you eat of the tree of good and evil? He's afraid you'll become as powerful as He is. He wants to keep you down. He's not out for your best!" And Eve believed him.

It was the devil who came to Jesus in the wilderness and tried to get Him to look to Himself rather than to His Father for food, position, and authority (Matt. 3:1-11).

So if the devil tried to tempt Jesus to doubt, you can expect he'll try for you, too.

How to Turn Doubt into Expectancy
Practically, we can do a number of things to turn doubt into expectancy.

Call doubt sin. Doubt is such a common experience among Christians that you can easily forget that it is not a problem, or a concern. The Bible says doubt is sin.

Jesus said, "Have faith in God" (Mark 11:22). When you doubt, you're disobeying the Lord's command. And any Sunday School kid can tell you that disobedience is S-I-N. What do we do about it? We confess it, and ask God for forgiveness.

If you're "trying to get over" your doubt, forget it. You never will. Because you're trying the wrong thing. You do not get over doubt; you treat it like any other sin: confess it and seek forgiveness. If you have a problem with impure thoughts, the Scriptures never tell you to try to do better. The Bible tells you to confess those thoughts as sin before God, and ask for His forgiveness and cleansing. And that's just the way to treat your doubt.

Get the right perspective. When Goliath came against the Israelites, the soldiers all thought, *He's so big we can never kill him.*

David looked at the same giant and thought, *He's so big I can't miss!*

The battle against doubt is basically one of keeping God's perspective on your problems, seeing them as God sees them. One of the best ways to keep perspective is to remember what God has done for you. That's why God told Israel, "You shall remember all the way which the Lord your God has led you in the wilderness these forty years" (Deut. 8:2). God knew that reviewing what He'd done for them would help them keep their eyes on Him during future hard times.

1. *Review how you started on this faith venture.* When the disciples were in the boat and saw Jesus walking on the water toward them, it was probably an upsurge of love and devotion to Jesus that motivated Peter to jump out of the boat, intending to walk to Jesus. But as he became aware of the waves around him, his eyes opened to "reason" and he reacted, *What am I doing here, anyway? Everyone knows that people are heavier than water! I must be out of my mind!* And he began to sink.

Just because there were waves all around him didn't mean Peter was out of God's will in jumping out of the boat. It only meant he needed to keep trusting as he walked across the waves to Jesus' side.

It's too bad someone wasn't there to say, "Now, Peter. Why did you get out here in the first place? Wasn't it because you love the Lord and wanted to express it? OK, maybe you chose a dumb expression, but your motive was right. So if God led you into the water, do you think He wanted to let you drown? Relax. He can get you through these waves to His side. Just keep your eyes on Him."

Don't doubt in the dark what God has shown you in the light.

Out of the major religions in the world today, all but one are based on the premise that if you keep the rules, good will be your lot in life. If you have troubles that's because you haven't been keeping the rules. Job's friends thought that when all his troubles befell him.

But it's on this issue of problems and trials that Christianity stands alone.

It's easy to operate with the mistaken idea that as God leads you in the Christian life, the immediate results will be peace, calm, and tranquillity.

The God who leads you is the One who said, "When you pass through the waters, I will be with you" (Isa. 43:2). Notice that this doesn't say *if* you pass through the waters. It's a basic, foregone conclusion that there will be deep waters for you if you're sticking with Jesus. God never promised you a rose garden. But He did guarantee His own eternal presence to meet every need, and to go with you step by step.

That's why James could say so confidently, "When all kinds of trials crowd into your lives, my brothers, don't resent them as intruders, but welcome them as friends!" (James 1:2, PH)

Problems are your friends? You're probably thinking, *It looks as if I've got a lot more friends than I thought!*

Often it's when you step out by faith that your troubles really start. But that doesn't mean that you discerned God's will incorrectly in your decision to step out. It only means you need to keep your eyes on Jesus to get you through the waves to the good He has in mind for you.

The Millers had decided to go to Colorado for a Christian conference from their home in Oregon, and had invited friends from Canada to go along. Both couples felt it was the Lord's will that they go, but as soon as the decision was made, troubles began.

For both of them the troubles were with money. Finances got tighter and tighter till it looked as if neither would have the money to go. The couple in Canada looked at the circumstances and backed out. They'd even gone so far as to send their kids to the babysitter who was going to keep them for the week of the conference. So they got the kids and brought them home.

But Dick and Sally Miller went back to the Lord to check their leading. They still felt He'd told them to go, so they asked Him to take care of the money, because they were planning to obey, expecting Him to supply.

The day before they were to leave for the conference, Dick's boss suggested an extra job Dick could do. Dick was a surveyor, so he went to the site, did the survey, and earned just the money he and Sally needed to go to the conference. They left for the conference with no financial worries. Just because the circumstances changed after they'd stepped out didn't mean God's direction had changed. He was only providing a bigger opportunity to let them see Him work. If you're doubting, review how you started.

2. *Review what God has done for you in the past.* David is a real pacesetter in this matter of not doubting. Part of that was because he built his new faith experiences on the foundation of what God had done in the past. Part of the reason he was so confident when he came up against Goliath was that as a shepherd he'd seen God help him kill a bear and a lion. So he assumed that this same God could give him the victory over this big Philistine.

One of my responsibilities when I was ministering to college students was to find a suitable place for our spring conference. I'd been looking and asking and trying, but I just couldn't come up with the right place.

This was a prime opportunity to doubt whether or not God was going to supply a place, but as I looked back on what God had done it just didn't make sense to doubt. The Lord had brought many students to Himself, had motivated them to want to grow, and had taken care of my family's needs so we could minister to them. Why would He stop now, since this conference was geared to helping students in their Christian growth? I'd seen Him provide places before.

Several students and I got together for prayer, and we came

up with a plan. We took a map and drew a circle on it that included every town within 50 miles of Maryville, Missouri, since this would be a reasonably central place for the people coming to the conference. Then we divided into twos and went to the towns in that circle to ask people about a conference grounds. We decided that we'd trust God and pursue any lead we got, no matter how ridiculous it seemed.

A student and I took off for central Missouri and started asking people about a conference center. We got many "I don't know" answers, but one man sounded positive.

"Sure, I know where you can ask. Why don't you drive down to the college at Tarkio and check there? They have conferences."

I knew right away this would never work, because my job was working with college students, and none of the colleges around us rented out their facilities during the school year. But we'd told God we'd pursue every lead, so we drove to Tarkio.

What I didn't know was that Tarkio was the only school in our area that was operating on the trimester basis instead of semesters, so their students would be on a two-week break at exactly the time we needed the facility for the conference. It turned out to be the nicest conference facility we'd ever used—new dorms, a new student union building, and only $6 apiece for the entire weekend.

The same God who had provided before had done it again.

3. *Review who Christ is and what He can do.* Surely the God who owns the cattle on a thousand hills can come up with the cash to pay your $40 phone bill. And the One who merely spoke to the waves and calmed them can surely give you good weather for your evangelistic picnic. He made a meal for 5,000 from five loaves and two fish. Surely He can multiply the food you need to care for your family till the next paycheck.

Remember who He is, His power, and His resources.

If you've tried confessing your doubt as sin, and reviewing what God has done, and you still doubt, the Bible has a special remedy for you.

Ask God to help; He can make you expectant. You've probably quoted James 1:5 a thousand times as a remedy when you needed wisdom. "If any of you lacks wisdom, let him ask of God, who gives to all men generously and without reproach, and it will be given to him."

But did you know that that passage was written for doubters who don't want to doubt? It was written to the person in trouble who doesn't know what to do.

Just ask God, James says. And God will give help liberally— generously. He won't make you feel silly for asking.

God is in the business of turning doubters into people of faith. He made Peter the denier into Peter the Rock. He can change you too.

Nothing pleases God more than a spirit of expectancy. So doubt your doubts. Expect God to work, and He will.

7

The Giver
Is the Getter

Jesus told His followers, "Give, and it will be given to *you;* good measure, pressed down, shaken together, running over" (Luke 6:38).

You want to have God working for you? You want to experience all He has for you by faith? One of the quickest ways to do that is to deposit some dollars with God, and see Him return them to you, with much more besides!

Janie had decided she'd had enough of the God stories she'd been force-fed at church, so she quit going. Since she didn't believe them anyway, why waste time? But her sister had different ideas for her, and one Sunday conned her into going to Sunday School on the pretense of needing a ride with Janie. It worked, and Janie wound up in a class where the discussion centered around some ideas that were new to her, ideas like God being loving, and that God cared about the details of her life. On the way home, she talked these ideas over with her sister.

"That's right, Janie," her sister responded to her questions. "God really does care about us, and He wants to give generously to us. In fact, somewhere in the Bible I think it even says that if we give to Him, He'll give us 500 times back what we gave! That's how generous He is!"

There is no such promise, but she had the right idea—God is generous.

Janie spent the next weekend drinking with her friends, and while driving home with the car full of people she had an accident and rolled the car. Miraculously no one was hurt, but the car was totaled. She'd have to be a pretty callous person not to believe that God had kept her alive, so to pay Him back she headed for church. As she sat in the pew, she thought, *I wonder about God. I didn't think He was real, but others like my sisters seem to feel it so strongly. And that accident maybe was no accident.*

So she decided to take a chance on finding out about God. When the offering plate came around, Janie pulled out $25 and put it in. "That's for You, God," she said. "If You are real, I'd like to see You return it 500 times over like my sister says You will."

Then things began to happen. The stock brokerage firm Janie worked for paid her $700 she wasn't expecting as a bonus for an efficiency idea she'd suggested earlier.

A friend she'd loaned $200 to months before suddenly called. "If you'll tell me where you live, I'll send you the money I borrowed." Janie was amazed. She'd given up on ever getting the money back. When the money arrived, the check was for $400 instead of $200.

In talking with her dad shortly after that, he inquired about a $4,000 debt she had. When she told him she still owed the money, he dropped the subject, but later put a check in the mail for the whole amount.

By this time Janie's head was spinning, and she realized that God was communicating to her in the very way she'd asked Him. She'd given, and He gave back just like He said. He was indeed real.

When God says, "Give and it *shall* be given to you," that's exactly what He means.

Giving is mentioned over 300 times in the New Testament. It's one of the most talked about subjects, running neck and neck with the Second Coming. And in teaching about giving, God doesn't command giving so much as He *commends* it. Make a faith deposit of money with God, and you'll see returns on that investment that will beat anything Wall Street could ever promise!

Who Benefits from Your Giving?

God is the one who tells you to give. But does He do it so that His needy missionaries can be fed, or that the hell-bound natives can get those Gospel tracts, or that your church can pay its light bill? No.

Giving is for your sake, because God gives to givers.

If you have trouble giving because you are afraid that you won't have enough left over to live on yourself, or because you have plenty to live on but you're downright greedy, cheer up! You make the best candidate for giving your money away there ever was. You probably don't give because you don't realize that the person who gets the most from giving is *you*.

That's right, and Paul's classic instructions to the church at Corinth concerning giving couldn't make this much clearer (1 Cor. 9:6-18). The whole passage is about giving. Now try to answer this question: "Who benefits most from my giving? The giver, the receiver, or God?"

Are you surprised? This passage of Scripture shows that all the receiver gets is his needs met. God does get something—He gets the glory, and thanks from the receiver.

The real winner is *the giver*. Paul states that God will love you; God will provide for you; He'll multiply your resources and your righteousness. (He'll not just add to them, He'll *multiply* them.) And we're not done. You'll be enriched, and you'll get prayed for.

So if you're basically greedy, take heart. You have every reason to become a hilarious giver. The more you give, the more God gives back to you. And we've already explored His resources, so you know you can never outgive Him.

Benefits of Giving

1. *You'll make the best financial investment money can buy.* Jesus gave His disciples this wise financial advice: "Do not lay up

for yourselves treasures upon earth, where moth and rust destroy, and where thieves break in and steal. But lay up for yourselves treasures in heaven, where neither moth nor rust destroys, and where thieves do not break in or steal" (Matt. 6:19-20).

Your Aunt Lucille dies and leaves you a tidy $10,000. You know a little about business, so you know that instead of just spending the money, you ought to invest it wisely. Then you can have your $10,000, and more besides. So what's the investment going to be? How about real estate? But buildings burn down. Or maybe diamonds? But they can get stolen. How about stocks? But companies can go broke. The crash of '29 proved that. Government bonds? But governments have been known to default. Look at New York City.

Giving, the Bible says, is laying up treasures for yourself—investments—in heaven. No thievery there, no fires, no governments failing, businesses bankrupting, or stock market crashes. You can't take it with you, of course, but if you're a giver, you can send it on ahead.

Giving is not only a no-risk investment, the returns are great. God promises that what you give will come back to you abundantly. Remember the promises of Malachi? "Bring the whole tithe into the storehouse . . . and I will . . . open for you the windows of heaven, and pour out for you a blessing until there is no more need. Then I will rebuke the devourer for you so that it may not destroy the fruits of the ground" (Mal. 3:10-11).

Has the devourer been hanging around your door lately? Maybe he's been devouring your cash by car troubles, or hospital bills, or bad investments. For givers, God promises to rebuke the devourer, so His protection will be on you and your assets.

Now this is not to imply that if you're a giver you can plan on never having hospital bills, repair bills, or other troubles, but the Scripture does seem to indicate a special protection on givers. So you see, you'll be getting returns on your investment you never planned on.

2. *You'll get a right heart here on earth.* Do you sometimes wish you were more concerned about the things of God? That you

had more of a heart to care about what God cares about? Jesus said, "Where your treasure is, there will your heart be also" (Matt. 6:21). If you're giving your money to God, your heart will be in the things of God.

That's why companies encourage their employees to buy shares of company stock; it's an easy way to motivate a man to give his best for the company. They know that where a man's money is, his heart is there also.

An economics professor at Iowa State University, who wanted to interest his students in Wall Street, came up with the perfect way to do it. He didn't assign them a term paper on it, nor ask them to give reports, nor threaten them with a test. He simply gave them $1,000 and let them invest it. He almost needed a referee before class every day to keep order as the students fought over who was to read the *Wall Street Journal* first to see how the stock was doing.

At South Dakota State University one year the Math Department hit on a solution to a problem with its tutoring program. Tutors were offered for the math courses, but students who signed up would not show up. So the department began asking every student who wanted tutoring for a $20 deposit at the beginning of the semester. Ten sessions were offered, and at each session the student attended, $2 was refunded. Attendance shot up. Where your treasure is, your heart is also.

If you want your heart to be in the things of God, put your money there, and your interest will naturally follow.

3. *You'll grow spiritually.* Jim and his wife were new at trusting God and giving to Him by faith, but they decided they'd take some of their money each payday and give it to the Lord's work. This was some step of putting God first for them, since their salary barely covered their needs as it was.

Jim was amazed at the results. He told me later, "For most of the five years of our marriage I've been a conniver, always trying to work things out on my own. In any two-week pay period I'd always try to figure out the bills a number of times, putting them down on paper, trying to come up with different ways to pay them.

I was always concerned about money and how we were going to make ends meet. That was me.

"But since we decided to give our money as a family, God has given me a spirit of peace about the money situation. I no longer feel a desire to sit down and figure out the bills because for the first time, we're committing them to the Lord and He's taking care of our needs."

God gave back to them financially for their giving. They're doing better now on 90% of their income than they did previously on 100%. More than that, God has given them a deep commitment and trust in Him. That's what I call spiritual growth. Givers indicate by their actions, not just with fancy talk, their desire for growing in God, and God blesses that desire. If you're desiring spiritual growth—to be more like God next year than you are now —a practical way to tackle that desire is to get out your checkbook and go to work.

4. *You'll get a welcoming committee in heaven.* No, I did not make this up. I found it in the Gospel of Luke, where Jesus is teaching about money and the use of it. "I say to you," Jesus stated, "make friends for yourselves by means of the mammon of unrighteousness; that when it fails they may receive you into the eternal dwellings" (Luke 16:9).

I believe the interpretation of this statement is this: If you invest your unrighteous mammon into getting people saved, they'll be there to welcome you into the eternal habitation, waiting for you in heaven when you go there yourself.

For some of us, Peter will open the gate of heaven, and we'll go in. Things'll be pretty quiet, and we'll venture around with a flashlight looking at the street signs, trying to find our mansion. Not a soul in sight.

But if you're a giver, you'll enter the gate, and a crowd will be waiting. It'll be a bands-and-confetti-throwing time, lots of cheering, and maybe even a chorus of "For he's a jolly good fellow."

"Who are all these people?" you'll ask.

One of them will come running up to you and grab your hand. "We never met," he'll begin, "but remember that $10 you gave to the Billy Graham Evangelistic Association? Well, I was looking for God, and heard the crusade on TV one night, and that's how I met the Lord. I checked the files here and found that it was your $10 that helped with that crusade. Thanks."

And another will chime in, "I came to Christ through that missionary your church sponsored. The files here say it was your gift that was supporting him when he shared the Gospel with me."

Plan your own reception! It's a "give now, get welcomed later" plan.

5. *You'll get out of debt.* How does that sound? Like the impossible dream?

Solomon said, "There is one who scatters yet increases all the more, and there is one who withholds what is justly due, but it results only in want" (Prov. 11:24). We live in a world that says, "Save and you'll have." But in God's economy the "standard operating procedure" is, "Give and you'll get."

I've seen this work numbers of times.

A couple I've known for years tell of the time when they were beginning in Christian work, and finances were low. Actually they were more than low, since they were $180 in debt. They'd prayed about what to do, and scripturally couldn't find a solution except to increase their giving, since God has promised that if you'll give, you'll get. So they wrote a check by faith.

Soon a check arrived in the mail for them, for $100, from a Sunday School class they'd been involved with on the East Coast several years before. The class didn't give to them regularly, but this particular time, a class member had come to the teacher with a check for $1,000. "The Lord has really blessed me," the person explained, "and I'd like to give this away. You probably know of some needy people. Why don't you divide it up and send it to them?" And my friends came to the teacher's mind.

Within a week the other $80 had come in, and the debt was cleared.

Another couple I met were just ready to start giving. They were ranchers, and had found the Lord in an exciting way. They had, with several other ranchers, become concerned about the fact that the little church in their area was really shabby. So the ranchers banded together and decided to build a nice new brick church. This is particularly amazing, since none of them were Christians.

When the building was finished, they decided to have some meetings in it, so they secured a speaker. Interestingly, the speaker they chose was a returned missionary, who came and simply presented the Gospel. Five of the key couples in the area came to the Saviour.

All five couples turned on to spiritual things, and when I met them, one man had decided to sell his ranch operation and go to Bible school. I turned to one of the other men and asked, "How about you? Why are you staying on the ranch?"

"I've prayed about doing what he's doing," he responded, "but I think the Lord wants me to stay on the ranch and support missionaries instead. The only problem is that I don't know any to support."

I hardly put that in the category of a problem, so I hooked him up with a missionary, and he started giving monthly to his support. A year later we met again and I asked him how it had been going with him since he decided to become a giver.

"You won't believe it, Russ." he said. "I've given away more money this year than I ever dreamed *anyone* could give and I didn't make any more money on the ranch than I did before, but somehow I'm out of debt. All I can figure is that God can stretch a dollar that's His in ways we'd never dream."

He was right. If you're in debt, you need to look to God to get you out, and make a deposit of money with Him to activate your faith.

6. *You'll have God prospering all that you do.* The Lord challenges His people to give, then makes a promise: "Because for this thing the Lord your God will bless you in all your work and in all your undertakings" (Deut. 15:10).

Having God bless all your works and all you take on sounds like a pretty good deal, doesn't it? That's making an offer you can't refuse!

In his book *A Spiritual Clinic*, J. Oswald Sanders has a chapter called "The Neglected Ninth Beatitude." Now most of us know the eight beatitudes, the "blessed are's," in the Sermon on the Mount (Matt. 5:3-10). But did you know there was a ninth? It's found in Paul's words to the Ephesian elders, as he refers to Jesus' statement, "It is more blessed to give than to receive" (Acts 20:35). Giving is the way to get God's blessing on all you do.

Stan found this out in an exciting way.

He's in the construction business, and right after Christmas 1974 business seemed to be moving at two speeds: slow and stop. January and February were the same; his money ran out and bills kept coming in. Stan and Mary prayed and the Lord revealed two things to them.

One was that they needed to be giving to their local church. They'd been faithful in giving to missionaries, but the Lord spoke to them about supporting their church also. This meant doubling what they'd been giving, but they decided to obey God and trust Him.

The second thing the Lord did was to lead Stan to give away the one source of income he did have. When work had slowed, Stan had gone to work for a friend in the painting business just to fill in during the financial crisis. But a young couple whom Stan and Mary knew moved to town, and were having a hard go of it. They were broke, expecting a baby, and the young man couldn't find a job. So Stan decided to offer his job to this friend as a deposit that God would provide something better for him. The friend was interested, and took the job.

No thousand-dollar contract appeared immediately, so Stan took on part-time remodeling jobs to help out, and waited on God. A contractor in town called one day, wanting Stan to redo some work on a barn that another carpenter had messed up. The contractor was so impressed with Stan's work, that he offered him another job—as an estimator and scheduler for his work crews—and the salary was higher than Stan had ever made before.

That's what happens when God decides to bless all that you do. Stan and Mary's double giving brought God's blessing on their work.

But Stan's story didn't stop there. His friend, who'd taken his painting job, had bills too. So he and his wife asked God to get them out of debt before their baby came, and as a deposit they decided to buy a new chain saw for a man who was opening up a Bible camp. The chain saw was a real sacrifice for Eddy and his wife, but they believed God meant His "give and you'll get" promises.

Besides painting, Eddy framed houses for a living, and he'd been working for another man. After they began giving, Eddy's boss decided instead to let him subcontract the framing he'd been doing. So, he was doing the same work, but for more money. When Stan saw Eddy again, Eddy had received enough extra money from the house he was framing to pay off all their existing bills.

If you want a blessing on your life, get teamed up with God. And a good way to do that is to give.

7. *You'll get a living, growing faith.* Faith needs works to come alive. The Bank of Heaven needs a deposit before it can return interest to you. And giving is the way to make that deposit.

When Paul was a senior at the University of Nebraska, he evaluated his finances, then stopped over to talk to me about it.

"You know, Russ," he began, "I figured out how much it's going to take for me to finish out the school year—tuition, books, personal stuff—and I have just enough to do it. But the problem is that I've also pledged $125 to missionaries. It looks like if I give that money away, I won't have enough to finish the school year. But I've decided to give the $125 and trust God that He'll take care of me."

Paul gave the money, and in a few weeks I got a phone call.

"I was home this weekend helping my Dad with a farm sale, Russ, and he decided to sell a horse and saddle we had there. He told my brother and me that he'd let us split whatever that horse and saddle brought. And my share was $120!"

I didn't ask Paul how God supplied the other $5, but I didn't really need to because there's no doubt He did.

It was exciting to see God supply Paul's need, but it was even more exciting to see Paul's faith grow as a result of this experience of trusting God. And Paul and his wife today are seeing their lives dynamically used by God to help other couples learn to trust God. Giving helps your faith grow.

Get Your Deposit in the Bank of Heaven

God gives to givers, and givers are getters. They get money, prosperity, blessing, and eternal rewards; and, most of all, they grow in faith.

By the way, giving money is so significant to God because giving your money is a way to give yourself. Though God has no real need for your money, He does have a desire for your heart, and getting your money is a way to get your heart.

If you try giving cash without giving your heart to God too, it doesn't work. You may have read in the papers about the man who took his church to court and sued for the $800 he'd given to them over the years. His complaint was that he'd given the money as a result of the pastor's promise that God would richly bless him, and he hadn't seen it happen. So he wanted his money back. *No one can purchase God's blessings or rewards.*

By the same token no one can refuse to give and realize God's blessing on His life.

Giving is a way to deposit on your faith, and to watch your spiritual life grow. You may start as the giver, but you'll wind up becoming the getter.

8

The Bible Will Keep
Your Faith Moving Ahead

Among Christians you'll find a variety of responses to the Bible. Some describe it as castor oil—bitter, but good for what ails you; then there's the Shredded Wheat approach—it's dry, but nourishing; or there are those who use it like Brylcream—a little dab'll do ya.

It's next to impossible to build a life of true faith without the Bible, because the Bible keeps you in touch with the resources of God. Faith without the Bible to guide it is like a destitute man who's found out that his family fortune is buried somewhere in the Appalachian Mountains. He might be able to find the money eventually by digging here and there, but how much easier if he'd just had a map!

Paul says, "Faith comes from hearing, and hearing by the *Word of Christ*" (Rom. 10:17).

God's Character

A Christian woman flying from Colorado Springs to Denver began talking about spiritual things with the girl sitting next to her. The girl responded, "Well, I know I should be more religious. I used to go to church a lot but then I got into skiing and enjoyed that more, so I quit."

"Tell me," the woman asked, "what was the God like that you gave up for skiing?"

The girl thought about that for a moment. Apparently this was a new idea to her. "My dad is a terrific man—one of the greatest you'll ever meet—but he's not much for going to church. And the church I was going to says that God'll send you to hell for not attending. So I guess the god I left was one who'd condemn a wonderful man like my father to hell for not getting bored in church once a week."

The Christian shook her head. "If that's the god you were serving, I'd give him up for skiing, too! But you ought to investigate the God of the Bible. I think you'll find that He's somebody worth giving all you have to."

Jesus said, "God is spirit, and those who worship Him must worship in spirit and truth" (John 4:24). How do you worship God in truth? By worshiping Him for who He truly is, rather than some image you've created of what He is or how He's going to act. And you need the Bible to help you discover what God is really like, because if you look only to circumstances or people's opinions you can really get confused.

Our world is full of people teaching false concepts of God. I'd like to have a nickel for every movie made in the last decade that depicts a preacher as either a wife-beating, murdering, immoral man who claims he's been called of God to attack those who oppose him, or a meek and mild pious saint whose life is bound up by one "thou-shalt-not" after another. And neither stereotype really represents the people of the God of the Bible.

You need to be able to cut through the mountain of philosophical garbage around today and go after God Himself. That's why you need the Bible—to worship Him in truth for who He really is. Because faith is reliance on someone else, your confidence in that Someone Else naturally increases as you get to know Him and see His trustworthiness.

God's Promises

When my daughters were eight and nine, they came up with their own idea for a Mother's Day present for my wife, Patti. They called it a "Promise Book." It was crayoned full of valentines and flowers, and each page had a promise written on it, like "I promise to wash the dishes" or "I promise to make my bed." The idea was that Patti should tear the promise page she was interested in and present it to the girls to cash it in on the service offered.

And that's what God has done for you in the Bible. When you have a need, you can go to His promise book, get the one that fits your need, and cash it in. Without the Bible, you don't know what those promises are when you need them.

While Daniel was a captive in Babylon, he was reading one day in the Book of Jeremiah. He noticed a promise that God had made to Israel concerning her captivity (Jer. 25:8-14; 29:10). He realized that the Lord had promised that the desolation of Jerusalem would last for 70 years. So he pulled out his pocket calculator, and figured out that 70 years had passed since they'd gone into captivity. He began to pray and trust God for deliverance. The books of Ezra and Nehemiah record the answer to Daniel's prayer. It was finding that promise that motivated Daniel to ask for deliverance (Dan. 9:2-3).

Discovering the promises God had made and learning to use them transformed my life of faith.

A few months after I'd become a Christian as a college student, I was drafted and shipped off to basic training. Those who have been in the service know that the atmosphere around a military base is about as conducive to being a growing Christian as the Pacific Ocean is to growing string beans. And I was drowning. I'd come into the military eager to maintain my Christian life, but before long all the temptations and opportunities to sin pressing in around me left me confused and wondering if I actually was a Christian after all.

It was in this spiritual fog that I landed in Fort Bragg, North Carolina to join the 82nd Airborne. The first morning I was there, a sergeant stood up and announced that there would be a Bible study at 6:30 Saturday evening in the Religious Center. It was like offering a steak to a starving man. That evening I went looking for the group, but by the time I found the center I was about 15 minutes late for the study. When I walked in, the men were already seated in a circle, and a lieutenant was talking with them.

He was discussing the need we have for the Word of God to bring us in contact with the power of Christ. Since what I'd been lacking was a big dose of God's power, that sounded good to me.

"Can anyone give me a verse that talks about what the Bible can do for us?" the lieutenant asked.

I looked up, surprised. I was raised in a church that was familiar with using the Scriptures, but that question was beyond me. I could have told him what I thought the Bible could do, or at best what I guessed the Bible said, but to actually pick out a verse, well, I didn't see how anybody could answer that one.

The lieutenant then pointed to the pfc. sitting in front of him, and the man immediately responded, "First Peter 2:2 and 3 talks about what the Bible can do."

I remember taking my Bible and opening it to the table of contents because I had no idea where the book of 1 Peter even was. Just as I located it, the lieutenant said to the pfc., "Quote it."

And he did: "Like newborn babes, long for the pure milk of the Word that by it you may grow in respect to salvation, if you have tasted the kindness of the Lord." I was amazed.

Then the lieutenant turned to one of the other men and asked him to quote a particular verse, and he did.

At that, I shut my Bible. It seemed to me I was among a group of minor prophets.

After the meeting the lieutenant talked with me privately and explained why it was that I saw such confidence in the lives of those soldiers. He made it clear that they were just like me, with the same desire to live for God, but that their spiritual hunger was being satisfied by the Word, while I was literally starving myself spiritually.

Then he pulled out a little booklet that had four Bible verses in it. "Private, I want you to memorize three of these verses by the study next Saturday night."

That week I memorized those verses. And one of them began

to change me. It was God's promise that He is faithful and will provide a way to escape temptation (1 Cor. 10:13). I'd come up against some of the same temptations to sin that I'd had before, and that verse would pop into my head.

"I've promised you that this one isn't too hard for you, Russ," the Holy Spirit would remind me. "And there is a way to escape. I will be faithful to you."

And as the Word of God got into me, I saw myself begin to grow as a Christian. I trusted God more because I was getting to know the God I was trusting. I found out what He'd promised to do, and began to claim those promises on my own.

The promises are there for you, but you can't benefit from them if you don't know what they are.

God's Perspective

A child is born without arms or legs; a young mother of four dies of cancer; a man is gunned down by an insane sniper. If you knew nothing of God and looked only at these circumstances, what could your possible reaction be but bitterness and despair?

You've probably had the experience of climbing aboard an airplane on a rainy, ugly day only to have the plane take off and in a matter of minutes find yourself above the storm, basking in the sunlight. So what's your conclusion about the day? Would you say it's stormy or beautiful? It all depends on your perspective, whether you're looking from the top down or the bottom up.

That's why Paul and Silas could sing praises to God in the middle of the night while in prison (Acts 16:25). And why Joseph, after being sold into slavery, could say to his brothers, "You meant evil against me, but God meant it for good" (Gen. 50:20). These men were looking at their life circumstances from God's perspective instead of their own.

An American POW who spent seven years in the Hanoi Hilton shared how God's Word gave Him God's perspective in a situation most of us would view as unbearable.

One Christmas during his captivity, the prisoners were allowed to receive Christmas cards that the Merrill Lynch Investment Company had sent them. In the card was a biblical message: "There is an appointed time for everything. And there is a time for every event under heaven—a time to give birth, and a time to die . . . a time to weep, and a time to laugh . . . a time to love, and a time to hate . . . a time for war, and a time for peace" (Ecc. 3:1-8). The Lord used that message to speak to the POW that his circumstances hadn't happened by chance; they were perfectly timed to accomplish God's purpose in his life. That perspective sustained him through his captivity.

From your own perspective you can't accurately determine what is victory and what isn't, because what appears to be a human failure often is God's perfect plan to produce ultimate success. Take Christ dying on the cross, for example. From a purely human view, this was the ultimate defeat. But from God's view it was victory over sin and death for the whole of humanity.

That's why Paul's double-talk actually makes good sense when he described himself "as sorrowful yet always rejoicing, as poor, yet making many rich, as having nothing yet possessing all things" (2 Cor. 6:10).

So which was he, rich or poor? Sorrowful or rejoicing? It depends on your perspective. And it's God's Word that can help you choose the right perspective on your circumstances.

Making God's Resources Yours

The God you serve has the habit of scratching where you itch. His Word wasn't meant to be a theological debate book; it was meant to make your life different. When God describes His Word, He calls it a mirror, light, bread, a sword, fire, a rock, and a hammer. I'm not sure you can get more everyday than that.

But for many Christians a missing link to being changed by the Bible is they never experience God speaking to them personally from His Word on a daily basis. They may read the Bible, but don't know how to hear a personal message from God to them from it. Maybe you're saying, "Yeah, that's me! But what do I do to change it?"

An easy way to start is to read a short passage every day, and mark a verse from the passage that seems to be significant to you in your present circumstances. Then jot down why that verse is meaningful to you, or how it could change your behavior.

Maybe the verse will be an encouragement to a different attitude toward someone who's been bothering you. Or maybe an idea to share with a non-Christian you're trying to reach. Or maybe a new thought about God's character that'll help you where you need it.

Go ahead and try. It doesn't have to be a big chunk you read, and the thought doesn't have to stagger Martin Luther. Just meet with God and let Him speak to you about Himself and your life. Then do what He tells you to do, or believe what He shows you. You'll find His resources becoming more and more effective in your everyday life.

Paul said, "I know *whom* I have believed" (2 Tim 1:12). And that knowledge of God and His resources made Paul a giant in faith. So get in the Bible to keep your faith growing; it'll keep your eyes open to the resources and perspective available to you from the God you're believing.

9

Praise Brings Changes

In the Dale Carnegie course I took a few years ago, the instructor challenged us to take those grouches in our lives—everyone has them—and respond to them with praise instead of grouching back. We all left class with the assignment to look for ways to praise the people who irked us.

When the instructor asked for a report on how we had done that week, one man raised his hand. "I tried praising the guy in my office who really bugs me, and here's what I discovered. It didn't change the old #$%¢& one bit, but it sure changed me!"

"Praise," one dictionary defines, "is *giving approval* to what is happening to us, good or bad, as it may seem."

If that's true, then things don't have to be good for you to praise God for them; you can even praise Him for the things you see as being bad that come into your life.

"In *everything* give thanks," Paul commands; "for this is God's will for you in Christ Jesus" (1 Thes. 5:18).

He also teaches that one result of being filled with the Spirit is *"always* giving thanks for *all things* in the name of our Lord Jesus Christ to God, even the Father" (Eph. 5:20).

David confirmed, "I will praise the Lord *no matter what happens* (Ps. 34:1, LB).

Most Christians you'll talk with have believed for years that when God does good for us, or blesses us, or makes us prosper, He should get praise. That's what Thanksgiving Day is supposed to be about, isn't it? God has been doing good things for you all year, so you thank Him for it. You're letting Him know you approve of what He's done. Just let Him give you a raise, or heal your sick child, or prompt Uncle Willie to leave you his cabin cruiser in his will, and God'll get praise.

But sometimes it isn't easy to give approval to the things that come into your life. Like the times you pray and don't get the answer you want. Or when the bills come in the mail and your husband walks in the door announcing he's been laid off his job. Or when you've longed for your son to leave his worldly life and come to Christ, but instead of taking up Bible study, he takes up drinking.

These situations can cause anxiety and unrest. Or they can mean peace and joy, if you're trusting God to work in them. The faith you need to experience God's peace in the midst of turmoil comes from praising God for the bad situation.

A woman in my Sunday School class shared that the challenge to praise God even for the bad circumstances came at a needy time for her. Her husband's job was waterproofing foundations for homes, so when the recession and the corresponding cut-back in construction hit, it struck them hard and their income went into a recession too.

To add to the problem, they'd been depending on rental income from some townhouses they owned to pay for their children's tuition at the Christian school they were attending, and the townhouses weren't filled. So it looked like the children might have to be taken out of Christian school, an unpleasant decision for them.

After the praise class, the woman got alone with God. "Lord, I sure don't feel like it, but You said to praise You for everything. So thanks that our business is going downhill. And thanks that the townhouses aren't rented and that we don't have the money to keep the kids in the Christian school. I'm going to praise You for all of this, even though I don't understand."

Next morning she was going over their checking account, and discovered a real surprise. She found an error that was in her favor. And the mistake involved enough money to carry the family financially for three months. Now the praise that went up to God wasn't any longer by faith; the Lord had worked.

But God wasn't done. The realtor who'd been handling their townhouses called with the news that he'd just rented out the empty one. And the people who had rented wondered if she would con sider accepting a contract to buy. So there was money for school as well.

Praising God for the bad situations frees Him to move in and work on your behalf.

One of my first discoveries of the power in this principle of praising God got results beyond what I'd ever dreamed.

One thing I've always wanted to do was to be a traveling evangelist to college students and speak on campuses. The problem with this desire is that students think they are notoriously intellectual, and I notoriously am not. So I put two and two together and concluded that there probably wasn't any way that desire could be fulfilled because I just didn't have the qualifications.

A few years ago I began to realize that God wanted my thanks for *everything* He was doing in my life, not just for the parts that worked out the way I wanted. So I decided to thank God for what He had made me, and that I wasn't an intellectual. Praising Him for how He had made me, even though I would have chosen it to be different, freed me from the frustration of what I wasn't compared to what I wanted to be, and really gave me God's peace.

But God had more than that in mind. After we had moved to Colorado Springs, my pastor called me into his office one day. "Russ, I have an idea for you. I've been thinking of a message you could preach to college students. Why don't you read *Future Shock* and *The Late, Great Planet Earth,* then put together a message on 'How to Prepare Your Life for the 21st Century'?"

I did. I've preached that message hundreds of times on campuses all across the nation. I've been on TV, radio, and in newspapers with it. I've taught college classes and even philosophy classes at the University of Massachusetts and the University of Minnesota with it. God has used it to bring many students to Himself. That's what I would call good results for an agriculture major who had read two books and began to praise God.

I think praise works like this because when you praise you open the door to supernatural power to produce results beyond what the natural could ever work out.

What You Need to Believe about God

Anyone who had even Psychology 101 in college might find himself getting a little nervous about this "being glad about the bad" attitude toward life. It might sound at first like a cop-out on reality.

That person can relax. God is not out to make you take a leap of faith off the Bridge of Reason in the matter of praising Him for everything. The psalmist tells you to praise the Lord with skill (Ps. 47:7). And you get the skill you need by getting to know God intimately.

God is sovereign. How much control do you believe God has? Do you believe He has power over all the earth? All of nature? All the governments and kingdoms? And that He can change and arrange any person or any circumstance that He desires? Do you believe that nothing, *nothing* touches your life except by His permission?

God is good. How good is your God? Do you have confidence that He doesn't play games with you, or shove you around like some cog in His Big Machine? Do you believe everything He does in the world—and in your world—is from His loving heart and for your total benefit?

God has all power. Do you believe He has more power than you do? So much power, in fact, that even if you mess things up, He can still turn them around to be all for good? Do you believe God is able to turn anything to good, even your failures, mistakes, and the lessons past sins have taught?

Without this kind of understanding of God's character, you would be like the Christian man in Kansas City who had gotten deeply in debt and finally decided there was no way out but to declare bankruptcy.

When a Christian brother challenged him to turn to God for help, he protested, "No, I can't. I got myself into this one. If I'd followed what God had wanted, I wouldn't be in this mess today. So it's up to me to get myself out of it."

George Sanchez, an experienced Christian counselor, observes that many Christians live their lives under the cloud of the "if only" syndrome. "If only I hadn't taken that trip, I wouldn't have been in that wreck"; "If only I'd gotten my husband to quit working so hard, he might not have had that stroke."

The "if only" syndrome comes from serving a God who is less than totally sovereign and totally good. With the God of the Bible, you can respond to the "if only" syndrome with, "Thank you, Lord, for the wreck, or Jerry's stroke, because You can and will work them for good for me. Nothing can stop You."

Just because the end of praising God is going to be all for your good, don't assume you have to understand all about how it's going to work out before you praise. Or that you have to know exactly what God is trying to teach you, or why it's all happening like it is. It seems that non-Christians ask, "Why?" and Christians ask, "What is God trying to teach me?"

You don't need answers to these questions as a prerequisite to praise, because you praise God by faith, faith that God will work it all out for good, so you don't have to try to understand everything that happens along the way.

Praise, you see, is not a way to avoid facing the realities of life. It's facing them head-on by faith.

What Praising God Will Do in Your Life
Praise releases God's power into your situation. Why doesn't God jump into every life circumstance and go to work? It isn't because He doesn't want to, or because He's lacking in ability or solutions. It could be that you've built walls around your life situations to keep Him from working. It may even be a wall of your will. You've decided just how you want the problem resolved, and if God in-

terferes, He might just work it out another way. Or maybe the wall is one of doubt, or fear.

How do you get those walls down to get God working in your life needs? How do you let go the control so He has freedom to do what He wants?

God inhabits—He lives in—the praises of His people (Ps. 22:3). So when you begin to praise God for those problem situations in your life, you are also bringing God into the middle of that problem. You've acknowledged His sovereignty in allowing the circumstance, and celebrated His goodness and power to bring it all out for good in the end. And that faith releases God's power to work in your problem.

A man at a faith seminar cornered me after the praise class. "Listen," he huffed, "I've heard what you're teaching before, and it wasn't in church! This is just psycho-cybernetics! Business executives learn their techniques from this all the time."

But I stopped him. "No, the difference between what I'm telling you and those think-yourself-rich courses is that they teach that the power is within you—and I'm saying it isn't. The power is in God, and praising Him releases His power."

A woman at a faith class shared that her child was in trouble with the law. She'd tried praying and pleading, but nothing helped. So she began to praise God for his behavior. That week her son and his wife came to Bible study, and the next week to church.

Her experience started a chain reaction because another woman in the group hearing the story decided to start thanking God that her kids didn't go to church even though she wasn't there very much herself. The next week she discovered that her daughter without telling her had decided to go to church after she'd gotten off the 11-to-7 shift at the hospital where she worked.

This woman's sister-in-law had the same concern for her children, so when she heard what God had done, she began to thank Him that her kids didn't go to church either. Before long she received a phone call from her daughter in Denver reporting that they had not only decided to start going to church, but were joining a home Bible study group.

God will work when His power is released into our life needs, and it's praise that releases that power.

That's the way it happened to Jehoshaphat and the people of Israel when they were being attacked by a horde of enemies (2 Chron. 20). They'd asked God's help and He assured them they'd win the battle without even fighting; they just needed to take their position and watch God win it for them.

Since they believed they weren't going to have to fight, Jehoshaphat told the choir to go ahead of the army singing praises to God. Very seldom do you ever hear of an army going into battle with the band in front. It'd be like sending the church choir instead of the Marines to storm the beaches. You couldn't be expecting much resistance if that's your strategy.

As they praised, the Lord set an ambush against the enemy and they were defeated without Israel so much as lifting a sword.

Praise released God's power into their problem.

Praise will always give you God's peace. One of the most profound secrets in the Bible on how to let God's peace keep your heart is tucked away in one of the most familiar passages you know. It's like hiding the key to your house in the lock. You may even have memorized the passage: Philippians 4:6-7.

"Be anxious for nothing," Paul said. Don't be full of care about anything. Don't worry. Don't be anxious. "But [here's the alternative to worry] in *everything* by prayer and supplication *with thanksgiving* let your requests be made known to God. And the *peace of God,* which surpasses all comprehension, shall guard your hearts and your minds in Christ Jesus."

You know the song, "Why worry when you can pray." But have you ever had a problem, prayed about it, and couldn't quit worrying? God says that there's a step beyond just asking His help. That step is to pray *with thanksgiving.* Ask His help, and thank Him that He is going to help. Thank Him for the situation, for the opportunity it gives you to see Him work, for Him to show His power and goodness. Thank Him for the way He is going to honor Himself and bless you through this problem you've got.

And the peace of God, Paul says, will keep your heart, your

emotions, and your mind. Praising God tells Him that you will let Him do what He wants in those circumstances, and in His way and time. It shows joyful acceptance of your circumstances from the hand of a good and sovereign God, who will work only good from them. That's liberating!

When Daniel was in Babylon, the jealous city officials now in the hands of the Persians, tried to wipe him out with a clever plan. They tricked the king into signing an edict that everyone had to pray to him only, knowing full well that Daniel prayed faithfully to God three times a day. They saw to it that the penalty was stiff enough to take care of Daniel for good; the violater would be thrown into a den of hungry lions.

The record states, "When Daniel knew that the document was signed, he entered his house (now in his roof chamber he had windows open toward Jerusalem); and he continued kneeling on his knees three times a day, praying and *giving thanks* before his God, as he had been doing previously" (Dan. 6:10).

How thankful do you suppose Daniel *felt* as he praised God, knowing that he was headed for the lions' den? The thanksgiving at that point probably came totally from his will, not from his emotions. But it didn't matter. Even if he didn't gush with thankful feelings, God honored his act of praise and saved him from the lions. He probably went into the lions' den with the peace that passes all understanding keeping his heart.

Praise allows God to change your situation, or to change you. Even though I could tell you dozens of stories of people praising God for problems and those problems being immediately resolved, praise cannot be a position from which you bargain with God. You can't say, "If praise is what it takes to get me out of this rotten situation, I'll do it." That's because praise is not a way to manipulate God, but *a way of life.* Praise isn't the source of your power; God is.

In His work with you, God always has two options. He can either raise the dead, or take away the sting of death. Sometimes he heals the mangled body, and sometimes he multiplies His grace to the afflicted one. He can part the waters before your feet, or else go with you through them. Either way when you praise Him, you free Him to work in accord with His perfect purposes.

In Carol's case, God changed the circumstances. Carol had moved to Colorado Springs with migraine headaches that caused such pain that she couldn't even lie down to relieve them. And they were becoming more and more frequent.

When she heard about the power released by praising God, she was excited. But to praise God for her headaches, especially when they caused her so much pain? She decided to try it, and began thanking God for His goodness and allowing the migraines.

One afternoon her vision began to blur, and she knew from experience that it was the first sign of an oncoming migraine. But instead of despairing that God had let her down, she began to praise Him for the headache. And the migraine never came.

Each time after that, when her vision began to blur, she began to praise. Gradually even the blurred visions began to disappear and the migraines were no longer a problem. She had praised them away.

For the Apostle Paul God did a different thing as a result of his faith. Paul had what he called a "thorn in the flesh." We're not sure what it was, but three times he asked the Lord to remove it, and God said no. His plan instead was to manifest a special degree of His grace and strength through Paul. So Paul responded, "Most gladly, therefore, I will rather boast about my weaknesses, that the power of Christ may dwell in me" (2 Cor. 12:9). Paul's praise to God for his "thorn" was the same as Carol's to her headaches, but God instead of changing Paul's circumstances, changed Paul.

With Job God did both. When he received the news that all his oxen and asses had been stolen, all his sheep had been burned up by a fire from heaven, all his camels had been taken by raiders, and all his children had been killed in a tornado, he responded by falling down, worshiping God, and blessing His name. As a result the Lord led him into a new depth of spiritual experience. When that was done, God gave him back all he'd lost—doubled.

When you praise God for problems, expect results. And the

results may be that God will change your situation, or else He'll change you.

It's hard to determine sometimes if praise comes from faith, or faith comes from praise. But either way, if you're out to live by faith, make a habit of praising God, even when things are bad. It'll release His working in your life, and you'll find the power and the peace of God permeating the way you live.

10

Obey Your
Way to Faith

A Christian man started a national chain of restaurants, and began with the policy of hiring only Christians. It didn't take long for him to change that practice. His reason was that the believers he hired didn't do a good job.

"I can't figure it out," he finally commented. "It must be that since salvation is free, they assume that everything else is too."

Not a very good commentary on the life-style of people who are supposed to be committed to Jesus, is it? It's the same attitude that Jesus was speaking of when He asked a group of His followers "Why do you call Me, 'Lord, Lord,' and do not do what I say?" (Luke 6:46) A disobedient Christian is a contradiction in terms. What you say about Christ being your Lord has got to match how you live. Righteousness is doing what is right.

Holiness in Little Things

A man of God from Judah was sent to King Jeroboam with a message that God was going to judge the king for his wickedness. When Jeroboam pointed at the man of God with a command that he be thrown into prison, the hand he had stretched out just dried up. God's power was obviously with this prophet.

But there was one problem. The man of God had strict orders

from the Lord *not* to eat bread or drink water in that place. When the king offered these things to him, he refused in no uncertain terms. But as he was going home, another prophet stopped him and announced that God had made a later revelation that it was all right for him to eat and drink there after all, and he invited the man of God to his home.

The second prophet was older, and of course wisdom and age go together, don't they? Our man of God obviously thought so, because without even asking God he went with the man. In return for his disobedience, God had him torn apart by a lion.

Little things don't matter much to us, but they matter a great deal to God. Paul understood this, and declared that his goal was "to maintain always a blameless conscience both before God and before men" (Acts 24:16).

When I lived in Nebraska, I was spending time with God one day in a park near my home, seeking the Lord for a message to preach at a conference that was coming up. I kept praying, but no answer came. I prayed some more, but still no answer.

On the way home, I changed my question. "God," I asked, "is there anything between You and me that's keeping You from being able to show me what message You want me to preach?"

"Yeah, Russ. That dirt," God seemed to say.

"The dirt?" I laughed a little to myself. "Now, God, about this message . . . "

"Now, Russ, about that dirt . . . "

A new office building was going up next door to my house, and beside the construction site was the biggest, nicest pile of black dirt you ever saw. I noticed my flower beds needed some good black dirt. It was Saturday morning, not a soul was in sight, and there was a wheelbarrow and shovel right beside the pile of dirt.

What would it hurt if I helped myself without asking? I thought. *After all, they came over last week and asked if they could hook their water hose up to my spigot, and they offered to pay me but never did. This will just even the score.*

So I loaded that wheelbarrow full of dirt, filled my flower beds, and returned it before anyone knew the difference. Anyone, that is but God.

So that morning as I prayed, I called it what it really was— stealing. And I asked God's forgiveness. The next day I went to the construction foreman and confessed stealing his dirt. It wasn't the easiest thing to do, but I knew the blessing of God on my life wasn't worth trading for a crummy wheelbarrow full of dirt. The man didn't know what to say. My conscience was now clear, and God gave me the message I needed.

I shared this experience once in a meeting, and afterwards a man came up to talk with me.

"Russ, my wife and I are headed for the mission field, I've got a wheelbarrow full of dirt too. When I was young, a friend and I broke into a liquor store in my home town and wrecked the place. No one could ever prove we did it, so I got off scot free. And I think God wants me to go back and make it right. The problem is, we did some $8,000 worth of damage. I can't come up with the money."

He decided that God did want him to make it right, and that he'd just have to trust God for the consequences. He went to see the liquor store owner to confess and offer to make it right.

The man couldn't have been more surprised. When the young missionary finished telling his story, the man looked up. "Listen, that was eight years ago. What's past is past. I'd just as soon you'd forget it."

"When a man's ways are pleasing to the Lord, He makes even his enemies to be at peace with him" (Prov. 16:7). This man pleased the Lord by not covering his sin, but by bringing it out into the light of God's forgiveness.

God is not wishy-washy. The God you serve is holy and righteous. He's the One who dealt with Ananias and Sapphira when they claimed they had given all their money to the church when they actually hadn't. They lied, and they died for it. The Old Testament records many people disobeying God, and the Lord punishing them. God is serious about sin. He has called His people to holiness, and He expects nothing less. What we call problems

God calls sin. As long as you deal with them as problems, you won't experience God's forgiveness, cleansing, and victory. You need to face up to your gossip, criticism, pride, lustful thoughts, lying, covetousness, or trying to get the best for yourself, and call them what they are—sin. God says that if you confess these things as sin, He will forgive them.

God Does Forgive You

If we had a contest to determine the most-often used verse in the Bible, it would probably come out to be John's "If we confess our sins, He is faithful and righteous to forgive us our sins and to cleanse us from all unrighteousness" (1 John 1:9). It's amazing to discover that when you confess your sin, God forgives you and forgets the whole thing.

After I took the Dale Carnegie course, a man I'd met in the class stopped by my house late one night. "I've got a friend in the car," he began, "and he needs some help. Would you talk to him?"

The friend, it turned out, did need help. He was living under a ten-ton load of guilt for sins he'd committed, and needed a good dose of confessing them to God and letting Him forgive. After he did, he raised his head, and beamed. "Wow! I feel cleaner than if I'd taken a good, hot shower."

That's a terrific feeling. And probably one of the most marvelous truths in the Christian life. A Bible study of college girls were discussing the first chapter of John when they came to the statement that the law came by Moses, but grace and truth came by Jesus Christ. The leader asked, "What do you think the difference was, then, between Moses and Jesus?"

The group was silent, and the youngest believer of them spoke up. "It looks as if Moses came to tell us what we should be, and Jesus came to forgive us when we aren't."

Have you ever tried to punish yourself for your sins by feeling guilty and miserable for a few days (more, of course, if the sin was worse) and *then* asking God's forgiveness?

You can try to earn God's forgiveness, but that is exactly what Jesus' death on the cross was all about. If you don't accept the forgiveness God has provided *by faith* but try to shape yourself up to deserve it, then you negate the effect of Christ's death. Jesus might as well have never gone to the cross.

Psalm 51 is the prayer of confession that David made after he'd committed adultery with Bathsheba, had murdered her husband, and had been confronted by Nathan. Now those were horrible sins. But listen to what David said. He confesses his sin, and then says, "Be gracious to me, O God, *according to Thy loving-kindness; according to the greatness* of Thy compassion blot out my transgressions" (v. 1). David didn't expect to be forgiven because he felt so bad about his sins, or because he was a first offender. He confessed his sins and expected forgiveness because God is loving and merciful. There's no end to God's mercy and love, so that means naturally that there's never an end to the forgiveness available to you.

Then he told God, "Wash me, and I shall be whiter than snow" (v. 7). David thought that when God forgave him, right that moment he'd be totally clean, just as if he'd never done anything wrong. Even after sins like adultery and murder, you say? Yes, totally clean. Because a short time later he told God that he expects to be used again to teach His truth. "Then I will teach transgressors Thy ways, and sinners will be converted to Thee" (v. 13).

Bill had an honesty issue to settle. As the train sped across Italy, he was struggling about what to do. He'd come to Europe on a summer missionary venture to spread the Gospel. But that morning as he traveled to Italy, the Lord had reminded him of a college debt he'd lied about.

During his freshman year Bill had accepted a scholarship from his church that was given only to those who had planned to go into the ministry. The scholarship was given with the stipulation that those who accepted it would be in the ministry for at least five years, or they would be obligated to pay the money back. After his first year Bill had changed life directions and had begun to work with an interdenominational Christian group rather than his church. He'd always rationalized his way out of paying back the scholarship on the grounds that he was ministering to people now, though not from behind a pulpit.

But God kept after him. So that morning he told the Lord he'd be willing to go to the college officials and try to make it right. "But you're going to have to work for me, Lord," he prayed, "because You know I'm in debt now and I sure don't need another debt added to that."

The train pulled into Venice, and Bill and another student began to explore the city. Passing a cafe, they overheard some young men speaking English and decided to meet them, hoping to share the Gospel with them. Bill struck up a conversation. "You guys sound like Americans. Am I right?"

Not only were they Americans, but they happened to be students from the very college Bill had attended. Amazed at the coincidence, Bill mentioned to them that he'd been thinking that morning about contacting the president of that college.

"You sure won't have to go far," one student replied. "He's sitting at that table right over there."

Bill told his story and the president was so impressed that he decided to cancel the debt. The same day Bill took care of his sin by faith, the Lord arranged a meeting in Venice and cleared the record.

When you ask God's forgiveness, you can expect Him to answer, and to begin working for you right away, though it may not work out quite as neatly as in Bill's case. You might find yourself having to pay.

God's Commands Are Not Burdensome

I asked a group of college students who were studying the truth that God's commands aren't burdensome, to come up with synonyms for "burdensome." They said it meant frustrating, tiring, sickening, a pain-in-the-neck.

Do God's commands ever seem like that to you? Do you feel like they cramp your style? You're obligated to obey them, of course, but if you had a choice you'd probably rather not.

We feel that way sometimes because we forget that God operates on the multiplication principle. Most any farmer will tell you that if you plant a bushel of wheat, you don't get a bushel back. You get more like 40 or 50 bushels. And for a bushel of corn planted, you'll harvest 400 to 600 bushels. God operates like that with you. For every inch of obedience you deposit with Him, He gives back a mile of blessing. You can be so busy focusing on what you have to give in obedience you may be forgetting to look at what you get back. God's nature being what it is, what you get back is much, much more than what you invest.

Some of the results you can expect from obeying God are a rich, deep fellowship with Him, a meaningful relationship with other Christians, an effective prayer life, opportunities to witness, fruitfulness in your efforts for Him, and a genuinely happy life.

If you only studied the commands God gave to Abraham, you might conclude it would be difficult to obey them. But just focus for a minute on the promise that came to Abraham as a result of his obedience to God's commands.

After the Lord came to Abraham in Haran and told him to go to a land that He would show him, God said the result would be that Abraham would become a great nation (Gen. 12:2). When he obeyed, God came to him again and said he would be the father of a *multitude* of nations (17:4). That's not a bad return for moving your family.

How difficult it must have been for Abraham to do what God commanded when he put Isaac on the altar, but after he did God said, "Because you have done this thing, and have not withheld your son, your only son, indeed I will greatly bless you, and I will greatly multiply your seed as the stars of the heavens, and as the sand which is on the seashore" (22:16-17).

In return for his son's life, God gave Abraham his son back, plus millions of sons and daughters, as the number of stars in the sky. A pound of obedience brought tons of blessing in return.

God plans obedience for your good, and His. He wants to give richly to you, and as you obey Him, you open the door to all kinds of blessings on your life that disobedient Christians never experience.

"Trust and obey," the song goes, "for there's no other way to be happy in Jesus, but to trust and obey." You can believe your way to obedience and obey your way to faith.

11

You Want God to Use You? Volunteer!

Have you ever envied those Christians God is using? They are the ones who are always leading people to the Saviour, starting Bible studies or evangelistic outreaches in their community, and who always seem to have stories to share about how they witnessed to this person or that.

Have you asked yourself, "How can I get in on that? Wonder why I want to witness as much as he does, but never see any results? What's the trick? Why does God choose to use Him and not me?"

It happens by faith. If you want God to use you, trust Him to, and volunteer.

That's what a young collegian did in Canada, and it produced exciting results. Rick was a Japanese-American who was part of a group of collegians I took through some of the camping grounds in Alberta to share the Gospel with Canadian college students who were camped there for the summer. The first day we witnessed Rick came back and reported that he'd led four people to the Lord. The next day it was two, and by the third or fourth day he'd led 12 people to Christ.

I called him over.

"Rick," I said, "this is really something. What's your secret?"

"I don't know, Russ," he answered. "I never had results like this back at Oregon State. Before I came on this trip, I told God I was available to Him and asked Him to use me to bring people to Himself. He must have said yes."

By the end of the trip 40 people had found the Saviour through Rick.

A woman I met at a church retreat agreed with Rick that God will indeed take volunteers, if they volunteer by faith.

She'd heard that her neighbor was in trouble and wanted to help. The neighbor's husband had been hospitalized with some sort of mental problems, and her son had just left for the Navy, so it was a difficult and discouraging time.

I'm sure that what she needs is to find Christ, the woman thought. But she felt inadequate to get involved with such a complex situation. She wasn't sure what to say or do. So she told God she would like to be used to reach her neighbor for Him. The Lord began to impress on her that she should prepare something on prayer to share with the neighbor woman. This didn't seem to make sense, because her need was obviously the Gospel, but the woman obeyed, and went to see her neighbor.

As soon as she walked into the house, her neighbor began, "I'm so glad to see you! You know my husband's in the hospital and my son's away in the Navy. And I just can't seem to pray, though I know this is what I really need to do."

So the ideas on prayer fit the need perfectly.

Two days later, the Christian called her neighbor again, and the first thing she said was, "When are you coming over again?" The Christian did, and led her neighbor to Christ.

Sometimes all God needs is a volunteer.

This shouldn't be a surprising concept to us, because Isaiah did the same thing centuries ago, and the Bible record is clear. The Lord asked, "Whom shall I send, and who will go for us?" God was looking for a prophet, a representative who would take His message to the people of Israel. Isaiah heard and responded, "Here am I. Send me!" (Isa. 6:8). And God sent him. He wasn't drafted —he volunteered. And that was good enough for God.

In an interview with an NFL linebacker, a reporter asked him what he felt made the difference in the success of the NFL teams.

The player responded, "I don't think the difference is ability. Really the teams are all pretty well matched. But some teams seem to have a greater desire to win, and that's what makes the difference."

Christians God uses don't necessarily have greater ability than the rest. Usability is dependent more on desire, and faith.

You Really Are Inadequate!

The big joke going around the college campuses a few years ago was the one about the woman who took her son to a psychiatrist because she thought he was suffering from an inferiority complex.

After a thorough examination, the psychiatrist called the woman into his office. "No, Mrs. Wilson," he reported, "your son doesn't have a complex. Actually he *is* inferior."

So if you feel inadequate about helping others find Christ or helping them grow in their Christian experience, relax. You really *are* inadequate.

The kinds of changes we're talking about making in people's lives have to do with giving eternal life to mortal men and if you feel confident that you can do that, you're wrong. Of course, you could present the message, then strong-arm somebody into praying a prayer, filling out a Bible study blank, or getting him to sit in a pew, but none of us is adequate to help him be reborn spiritually.

That's why if you rely on salesmanship, you'll get what salesmanship can produce. If you rely on cleverness and intellect, you'll get what intellect can produce. But if you rely on God, you'll get what only God can produce, and that is men and women changed for all eternity. Converted. Lives turned around and going in a completely new direction.

God isn't looking for smart, gifted, musical, well-dressed, intellectual Christians to use. Those aren't his prerequisites. He's looking for those who are willing to be His vessels, to do His work His way and trust Him for the results. You don't have to be smart, or clever, or aggressive to do that. You just have to be available and trust Him.

When I was stationed at Fort Bragg, some other Christian soldiers I'd met shared my concern about witnessing. We really wanted to lead people to Christ. So we came up with a plan. Five of us piled in a car every Saturday and drove back and forth between Fort Bragg and Fayetteville, the nearest town. Naturally we found soldiers hitchhiking along that road, trying to get into town, so our plan was to pick up anyone we saw alone and share the Gospel with him all the way to town. Then we'd turn around and drive back and look for a soldier going the other way, so we could pick him up and preach. We figured this had to be pretty effective because with five to one odds, what one of us couldn't answer surely another could.

We never led anyone to Christ on those ventures. We had a lot of good experience witnessing, but no one ever trusted the Saviour. As I look back, I wonder if it was because we were trusting in each other and the five to one odds rather than in God. We were adequate, or so we thought, and it didn't reap eternal fruit. We reaped what we could produce.

Several years later my wife and I were in Europe. On a train to Italy we shared a compartment with Bill, a Christian student we knew, and a professor of law at the Athens Academy. As we got to know the professor, we turned the conversation to spiritual things.

The more we discussed things with him, the more impressive he became. He spoke seven languages and when we shared verses from the New Testament, he told us that he'd read them in the original Greek, which none of us had ever done. He was well-traveled, well-read, intelligent.

Our friend Bill finally spoke for all of us. "When I hear your ntellectual background, professor, you really make me feel inerior."

"Don't feel that way," he quickly responded. "You have me licked by your faith."

When you're relying on God by faith to reach others, you can lose on the grounds of intellect and still win the battle.

In God's book, when you're weak, then you're strong.

In my church we were having people from the congregation

give testimonies during the morning worship service of how they had found Christ. I was responsible for lining up the people who would share, and one whom I chose was a single girl. She didn't come across as being tremendously confident as a speaker, and I knew she'd have doubts if I asked her.

When she got up and spoke, the Spirit of God obviously took over, and of the testimonies given, hers was the only one that drew questions from the audience afterwards.

A man came up to her and said, "You know, when you spoke, it was like you were telling my life story, and I'm right where you were just before somebody gave you that little book about how to receive Christ. Do you think I could get one of those books so I could receive Christ too?"

The couple who had brought the young man to church were amazed. Even as they had invited him, both had thought to themselves that it probably wouldn't do any good.

The girl explained to me later, "I just asked the Lord to use me, and He did."

So if you feel inadequate to help others spiritually, don't let that keep you from volunteering. After all, if you were adequate and God worked, who would get the credit? So praise God you're not sufficient, and raise your hand to volunteer.

God Supplies the Tools

God didn't tell you to go to the whole world and preach the Gospel and then send you out empty-handed to do it. If He hadn't supplied the resources to do the job, you would have been empty-handed, because we've already settled that our human resources aren't much in doing supernatural work.

God has equipped you with the Bible and the Holy Spirit, and those two are a winning combination spiritually.

When a hammer hits you on the head, you know it. When you stick your hand into the fire, it gets burned. That's what the Bible calls itself—a fire, a hammer, a sharp and powerful sword. When these tools are used, they get results. God says about His Word, "It shall not return to me empty, without accomplishing what I desire, and without succeeding in the matter for which I sent it" (Isa. 55:11).

John, a non-Christian, was a tennis player at Oklahoma State University when his girlfriend shared with him the Bible verse, "You must be born again" (John 3:7). John discussed it with her, then also talked to a minister about its meaning, but the language wasn't familiar to him and he just couldn't seem to understand this verse.

A few days later he was getting ready for an important tennis match. As he was dressing in the locker room, everywhere he looked he could see, "You must be born again." This was a little frightening, so he hurried out on the court.

The match started, and in the middle of one of the games, John's opponent hit a high lob ball over the net.

John remembers, "I looked up for the ball, but couldn't see it because all I could see was 'You must be born again' in the sky. I missed the ball completely and it hit me on the head.

"The coach ran on the court and asked if I was OK. He figured the sun maybe had blinded me. I couldn't tell him what my problem was, but I knew then and there I was going to see that pastor again and find out what this 'being born again' stuff was really all about. The truth of that statement had me totally and I couldn't escape it."

Intellectual arguments or philosophical reasonings on the Gospel would never have stuck in John's mind like that. Nowhere does God ever promise to bless our reasoning power, but He does promise to give power with a capital "P" wherever His Word is used.

When I was out witnessing with a friend at Lincoln Air Force Base, we decided to go back and see a non-Christian we'd talked to on a previous visit. I was looking forward to it, because when we'd left the man the week before, my friend had said to him, "Just let me leave this verse with you to think about." And he'd quoted a Gospel verse.

When we found the airman, he came up to us eagerly. "I've been hoping you guys would come back," he said. "That verse you gave me has been going over and over in my mind, and it's really been bugging me."

Notice *whose* word stuck in his head—God's. Because where His Word is used, God blesses and reaches people. So become a sower of the Word. It's one of the most effective tools God has given you to help people find Him and grow in Him. When a hammer hits you on the head, you feel it!

The Holy Spirit will go to work on the inside while you work on the outside. You've got the Bible as your resource, and you've got the partnership of the Holy Spirit. With those two, it's like going into the manufacturing business with all the machinery you'll ever need and Standard Oil backing you financially.

With the Holy Spirit as your partner, you've got super-natural power to do a supernatural job. He's at work inside people, convicting them of sin, softening their hearts, showing them what's true, motivating them to the things of God. And He's at work in you, guiding you, telling you what to say, using what you do to accomplish God's purpose.

This is what Jesus meant when He said that when He sends His sheep out, He as the Good Shepherd goes ahead of them. And how He does this is in the person of the Holy Spirit.

Becky found out that God's work is a whole lot easier in partnership with the Holy Spirit. When Becky became a Christian, she changed completely. Her new life was so great that she was really concerned that all her old friends know about Christ. So she went after them with both barrels blazing. But the results weren't what she hoped for.

So as she was going home one weekend she prayed, "God, You know I'm going to see Carol this weekend, and I'm really concerned that she come to know You. But I want to give this to You and let You work it out Your way."

The Lord impressed on her that she shouldn't even try to witness to Carol. Instead, she should just relax and be friendly and see what God would do.

They got together, and Becky didn't bring up the subject of her new relationship with Christ.

Finally Carol, apparently unable to stand it any longer, blurted out, "Tell me about that God thing you've got. Everybody warned me you'd try to cram it down my throat, and I was all set to resist, but since you haven't even mentioned it I guess I can admit that I really want to hear." And Becky had a wonderful time explaining the Gospel to her.

One thing that's clear about working with the Holy Spirit: don't try to predict *how* He'll work; just expect Him to.

It's easy to begin to think you can read where the Spirit is working and where He isn't, and it's also easy to be wrong.

Several years ago I was speaking to an evangelistic meeting in the girls' dorm at a small Midwestern college. The subject was, "Religion—is it worth your time?" After the meeting, I met with a small group of collegians and talked about how they felt the ideas related to them. From the vibes I picked up in the conversation, there were three who seemed very interested, so I said, "It looks as if some of you in this group are thinking you'd like to respond to Christ. So out of courtesy to you, why don't we all bow our heads and those of you who want to can pray and ask Christ into your lives." So we all bowed our heads and I led in prayer.

After everybody raised their heads, I started around the group. I asked the first girl if she'd prayed, but she said no; she wasn't sure it would work. The fellow next to her said he'd invited Christ into his life a few years before. And the two I'd picked out as the eager ones both said they hadn't prayed, and didn't want to. The young man next to them said he wasn't sure it could be that easy. I'd had the group rated, and I rated it all wrong. The ones who looked so eager to me weren't eager at all.

But the Spirit still had worked, just not as I'd expected.

I looked over at the last two people in the circle, and inwardly shook my head. Both were obviously deep into the hippie lifestyle, and I could hardly see one face for all the hair. But I had asked everyone else, so I decided the only polite thing to do was to include them.

Maureen looked up. "I've always thought that to get to God you had to reach out for Him." And she stretched her hands toward the ceiling. "But when you were talking tonight I saw that it's just the opposite; God is reaching down for me! And when I realized that, something happened inside me."

I looked over at Court, her boyfriend. He looked up and shook the hair out of his eyes. "Yeah, I prayed," he admitted.

A half hour later as we were closing the room to go home, Maureen and Court were back.

"All day long we've been going around campus telling everybody, 'The Jesus Creeps are having a meeting tonight,' but we just wanted to say thanks for being patient with us."

Sometimes when the Spirit is working, you don't see the results until much later.

I was speaking on the campus at Kent State University when a man came up and shook my hand. He looked familiar, but I couldn't place him.

"I'm Dave Johnson, Russ," he introduced himself. "It's Dr. Johnson now, but we were in basic training together at Fort Chaffey, Arkansas. And you shared the Gospel with me there." He told me word-for-word what I'd said to him some 17 years before.

"I didn't show much interest in the Gospel back then," he continued, "but what you said stuck with me. And I found the Lord a year and a half ago."

So even if you don't see the results till years later, the Spirit is still working, even in ways you don't expect.

The Bible and the Holy Spirit, God's resources to you to help you reach others—supernatural tools to do a supernatural task.

Start Where You Are

All God asks is that you use His resources, and volunteer by faith. The next step is to start where you are with whatever you have and do what you can, and watch God multiply it.

That's what a businessman did when he found he had a 45-minute layover at the Dallas airport. He realized it wasn't much time, but his chief desire was to see God use his life. So he started with what he had, a pocketful of Gospel tracts.

He stuffed his business card into each tract, then went around the airport offering them to people saying, "This little booklet explains how a relationship with Christ can change your life. I've had that experience, and it's really changed me, and I'd like to share it with you. If you'd like to discuss it further, I'll be sitting right over there."

When he ran out of tracts, he sat down. Before his plane took off, people were lined up waiting to talk to him about the Lord. For weeks afterwards he received letters from people he'd met at that airport, wanting to know about Jesus.

That's a simple plan, but he used what he had and expected God to respond to his faith and multiply his efforts.

An older couple I once met did the same thing and saw God use them. Because their children were grown, their great desire was to go into full-time Christian work. So for two years they prayed and asked God to open up an opportunity.

After two years of praying, both of them decided, "If we're really trusting God to use us in Christian work, why don't we start right here?" So every Sunday afternoon they began to go out and witness in the neighborhoods in their town.

One month after they started their Sunday afternoon evangelism sessions, they received a call from the director of a Christian camp inviting them to come and work full-time on the camp staff.

They started where they were and did what they could by faith, and God multiplied it.

You may be one of the many Christians who really wants to be used by God to reach others for Christ. How does it happen? Not by intellect or ability, but by faith. Look to God as your resource, and make a deposit by stepping out and trying something, trusting God to multiply your efforts. God welcomes volunteers who trust Him to use them.

12

Keep on Trusting
When the Mountains Don't Move

Sometimes you step out by faith, you believe God, and the mountains just don't move.

Chuck Sears called me one day and sounded a little disheartened.

"I just don't understand it, Russ," he began. "This was all working so good for me there for a while. After I took the faith class, I gave some money as a faith deposit, and God gave right back. I gave again, and the same thing happened. But this time when I made a deposit, nothing, and I mean nothing, happened. Does this only work part of the time? What went wrong?"

Chuck probably felt just like the children of Israel when Moses took them out of Egypt. They stepped out by faith, and wound up in the desert.

Now, how do these spiritual "deserts" fit in with what the Bible promises?

The psalmist said, "No good thing does He withhold from those who walk uprightly" (Ps. 84:11).

He won't withhold anything good if you're trusting Him? But what about when it looks as if He is withholding? Are you to conclude that you must not be upright enough, and give up on expecting God to work?

Not at all. Jesus promised, "And everything you ask in prayer, believing, you *shall* receive" (Matt. 21:22). And He means what He says.

So if you're believing God, whatever you've asked Him for is yours, be it a need, a concern, or a desire. You can expect it on the basis of God's inherent goodness and love. A girl I know summed it up this way, "The Giver delivers!"

When it looks as if God isn't coming through on His promises, you can't assume He's going to withhold good from you. He never withholds, but sometimes *postpones* the delivery of His blessings, if by a postponement He can bring you greater good in the end.

A fantastic section in the Old Testament explains God's view on Israel's 40 years in the wilderness. He tells exactly why He postponed giving them the Promised Land, and His perspective may give you the understanding and hope you need to keep on trusting, even when the mountains don't move.

God Makes You the Person He Wants You to Be

"You shall remember all the way which the Lord your God has led you in the wilderness these forty years, that He might humble you, testing you, to know what was in your heart" (Deut. 8:2).

In the wilderness God turned a beaten, disheartened bunch of slaves into a nation of conquerors. But He didn't do it by having them up for calisthenics at 5:00 A.M., or by target practice on the bow-and-arrow range. He did it by re-working their character, by changing what was inside them. The testings in the wilderness made them into the kind of people God could use and bless.

Sometimes God has to wait with His answers till He can purify your heart of the lust, greed, or other wrong motives that keep you from really being His person in the way you want to be.

James explains, "You ask and do not receive, because you ask with wrong motives, so that you may spend it on your pleasures" (James 4:3).

When Patti and I were first married, we decided to give $75 a month to the Lord and His work. We were working for a Christian organization at the time, and after a month and a half of giving, we got a letter from the office.

They had decided to change the way we were being paid, and our income dropped to $88 a month plus room and board. It didn't take long for us to figure that if our income was $88 and our giving $75, that only left $13 a month to live on. Now granted, we were newlyweds, but even living on love takes more than $13 a month.

We had a decision to make: should we cut our giving, or go ahead and give, and trust God to meet our needs? We prayed, and felt God wanted us to give and trust Him to supply for us. And we saw God do that in some pretty miraculous ways, as people we didn't even know began giving to our support.

So the next year we raised our giving to $100 a month—by faith. The next year to $150 a month. And the next to $200 a month. And the next to $300.

By the sixth year of our marriage, we were giving $325 a month. At the time that was 50% of our income.

Then during that sixth year, God stopped delivering.

We would give and pray just as before, but no money would come in. And we started going in debt. I remember the month I couldn't make my car payment, and had to write the bank and tell them I didn't have the money.

This went on for six months, and we didn't know what to do. We were living by faith just as we'd always done, and we had all God's promises to givers, but God just wasn't doing what He'd said.

It took a while, but the Lord finally was able to get through to us why He wasn't blessing. He had trouble telling us because His reason was one I didn't want to hear. In the midst of those years of seeing God reward our faith, subtly in my own heart giving those large amounts had become a source of pride.

So to purify us, God wanted us to take a step that really hurt our spiritual pride; He wanted us to cut the amount we were giving. As soon as we did, our income went back up. We got out of debt and God again began to prosper us financially.

God will sometimes postpone His blessing to get a chance to purify you. When He does, be confident that He'll discipline you like a father does his much-loved child. It won't be like a drill sergeant disciplines a private. God's motive is solely for your ultimate good. You'll find His discipline will result in a heart more like His, and besides this you'll receive what you were trusting Him for.

God Reminds You of Who Is the Resource

God told the Israelites to beware "lest, when you have eaten and are satisfied, and have built good houses and lived in them, and when your herds and your flocks multiply, and your silver and gold multiply, and all that you have multiplies, then your heart becomes proud, and you forget the Lord your God . . . and you may say in your heart, '*My* power and the strength of *my* hand made me this wealth' " (Deut. 8:12-14, 17).

God is out to protect you from building on the wrong foundation, one that will eventually crumble beneath you. Sometimes continued smoothness in your walk of faith can lead to trust in self-righteousness (*"I'm* victorious all the time; why aren't *you?"*) or else trust in a system instead of in God.

Making a deposit with God and seeing Him respond to your faith could get you into the same trap that caught Joe.

Joe overheard a co-worker telling how he'd just won $200 in a lottery.

"It was so easy," the man explained. "See, today is the 29th, and I'm 29 years old, and this morning in the mail I got a bill for $29, so I figured I'd stumbled onto something. So I went right down and got number 29, and I won!"

It sounded good, and so easy.

The next morning, Joe woke up earlier than usual, and when he checked the clock, it was 5:00 A.M. As he was getting dressed, he noticed he'd left five nickels on the dresser the night before. And as he got on the bus to go to work, there were five people on it, and it made five stops before Joe got off.

Suddenly it hit him. "I must have found my lucky number!"

So he raced to the bank, took out his life savings, and went down to the track to put it all on the #5 horse in the fifth race.

Sure enough, the horse came in fifth.

It's not a surefire system that gives you victory, it's God. And He doesn't call us to gamble, but to have faith *in Him.*

God is out to help those who admit they can't help themselves. He's not trying to raise up self-reliant or self-confident people. God will do what He needs to keep you plugged into the right source.

Myron was working in Alaska when he heard about a job opening that sounded as if it was made for him. But the job fell through. And Myron was left with no employment and a family to support.

He and his wife sat down and looked over their finances.

"It looks to me," Myron concluded, "that we can make it for two and a half to three months at the most without a job."

So he started job hunting, but it wasn't until the day their money ran out he found a new job.

As he looked back, Myron concluded, "I think God didn't supply a job before the three months were over, because even though I was praying, I was looking to myself and that money in the bank as our resource. I think now I'd probably have gotten a job a lot sooner if I hadn't decided to rely on myself as long as I did."

When the children of Israel went to take Jericho, God told them to walk around the city for seven days. Now this plan probably was not so much to frighten the people of Jericho as it was to make sure there was no vestige of self-reliance left in the Israelites.

Can't you see them dragging back to camp after the fifth or sixth day of marching? They were probably physically shot, and the city walls looked bigger every day they marched around them. Even those who'd come up with an alternate plan of attack in case God's shouting plan didn't work must have thrown it out by now. They were most likely either too tired to try it, or too aware of the difficulties to think it would work. The choice came down to God working, or a disastrous defeat. And that was the necessary prerequisite for God to do a great miracle.

In God's mind, a little bit of faith in the right source is better than a washtub full of will or a ton of determination.

God may be postponing His answer to remind you of who is resource.

God Changes the Results of Your Faith into Greater Things

God's plan for the Israelites was to change the results of their faith into something much bigger than they'd ever imagined. The Israelites probably would have been willing to settle for a land free of Egyptian domination, but note what *God* had in mind for them.

"The Lord your God is bringing you into a good land, a land of brooks of water, of fountains and springs, flowing forth in valleys and hills; a land of wheat and barley, of vines and fig trees and pomegranates, a land of olive oil and honey; a land where you shall eat food without scarcity, in which you shall not lack anything; a land whose stones are iron, and out of whose hills you can dig copper" (Deut. 8:7-9).

Sounds like something out of an Arizona land promotion deal, doesn't it? Almost too good to be true. But that's what God wanted to give His children. And to do that, He needed to postpone His blessing so He could not only give them their desires but much more besides.

That's the way it happened for a family in Newton, Iowa too. They were getting too cramped for their house; the kids were growing and the house wasn't. So they planned an addition with a drive-under garage and a recreation room on top.

But nobody was available to come and dig the garage. Summer turned into fall, and the winter freeze was approaching so that the digging would be impossible. Everything they tried to get a digger to come didn't work.

A builder friend from a nearby town heard about their problem. "This is the most ridiculous thing I ever heard of, not being able to get someone to dig that garage for you. I'll send one of my men down to do it."

But as the family prayed about it, they had no peace about their friend bailing them out. They'd been asking God to get their addition underway, but He seemed to be blocking everything they tried. So they decided they had no choice but to wait on God.

As it turned out, God was postponing His help because His answer was bigger than they'd ever dreamed.

By spring, the Lord had given them the idea of moving to a different house instead of remodeling. And He consequently provided for them not just another house, but a property on the edge of town with a much bigger residence, and 20 acres of land. They had a big garden, a fishing pond, and animals for the kids. That postponed blessing turned out to be better than they could ever have come up with on their own.

Maranatha Bible Camp in Nebraska was built as a wilderness retreat, so when the government decided they were going to route Interstate 80 right on the edge of the camp, it looked like a disaster. After all, who's ever heard of a wilderness camp with a superhighway going by it?

So Christians began to pray and trust God to change the government's plan. They even hired a former lieutenant-governor of Nebraska to represent them in court on the matter, but nothing helped. The highway was going through. It looked as if God had withheld.

But that's because God's plan was much better.

When the highway was going in, it turned out that the builders needed sand to construct the interchanges, so they worked out an agreement with the Camp Director to get the sand from the campgrounds. And in return, they graded the hole that was left into a beautiful recreational lake that has greatly enhanced the ministry of the camp.

Plus, the highway cut right through a nearby farm in such a way that the farmer no longer had direct access to a part of his land, so he decided to sell it to the camp at a reasonable price. So besides the free lake, the camp expanded its facilities and increased its ministry. Not a bad return for waiting on God to fulfill His promise.

Russ and Doris realized that they needed to be spending more time together as a family, so they both decided to trust God to meet this need. They envisioned a lazy summer together with their kids, or maybe a week's vacation away from it all, because they'd been too busy during the school year to really be together much.

They trusted God by faith to meet the need, and then the roof caved in.

A group of teenage singers performing at the church camped out at their house. Then relatives came and spent a week. They were barely out the door when friends who had moved from Germany called. They needed a place to stay while they house-hunted in Colorado Springs, so they moved in for a week with their children. And just as that family left, a woman Doris had helped in Bible study called. She was in the hospital with a fractured jaw after her alcoholic husband had beaten her up. She needed a place for herself and her three kids to stay. So Russ and Doris opened their home, and for the next six weeks they took care of that family. The injured woman had her mouth wired shut and one of the children was a six-month-old baby, so it was no easy task. The woman had no income, so Russ and Doris took on her doctor bills, providing financially for her family as well as their own.

Some answer to a prayer of faith for more time together as a family! It looked as if God had let them down.

When the family moved out, Russ and Doris realized that through the circumstances God had answered their request, and more.

"We couldn't believe all the family time we had once Nancy left," Russ said. "Caring for that extra family forced us to get organized, so we wound up having a lot more time together just because we were more efficient at running the household."

During the six weeks of pressure, they'd unconsciously given up TV, simply because they didn't have time for it. Once their family was alone together, they found that the time they'd previously given to TV could really be used to enrich their family life.

God had not just given them a week together like they'd planned. He'd revamped their whole life-style to make them closer for the long haul.

Consistent with His generosity, God saw to it that a check for $500 came in the mail from a relative's estate. It more than made up to them for the money they'd spent on the needy family.

God never withholds the blessings you're trusting Him for, but He may postpone them if by that postponement He can purify your heart, keep you looking to the right resource, or give you more than you could ever dream or think of asking for yourself.

When you can't seem to get a trickle out of the river of God's blessings, expect it anyway and wait. The blessings are just building up behind the dam, and when God opens the flood gate, you won't know what hit you.

Faith Is the Way to Experience All God Has for You

God has called you, His child, to a rich, full life of victory and success. It's a life of met needs and fulfilled desires. But His plan is not that you strive for these results yourself, but rather that you look to Him to give them all to you. He wants to be the resource of all you need.

If you trust Him to give to you, and commit yourself with a faith that acts, you'll see God return your deposit of faith over and over again.

"Without faith it is impossible to please Him, for he who comes to God must believe that He is, and that He is a rewarder of those who seek Him" (Heb. 11:6).

Get to living like the child of the King that you are. Come to experience all God has for you, by faith. You'll find out in practice that God is more generous than you think.

God can make it happen!

Inspirational Victor Books for Your Enjoyment

Inspirational Victor Books for Your Enjoyment

D